IMAGES OF ENGLAND

BIRMINGHAM
THEATRES & ENTERTAINMENT

IMAGES OF ENGLAND

BIRMINGHAM
THEATRES & ENTERTAINMENT

PATRICK BAIRD

The
History
Press

Frontispiece: Theatre Royal, New Street, 1805. From a print published
by T. Woodfall of Villiers Street, London. This was the second
theatre in New Street. The original had been built in 1774 but was
destroyed by fire and rebuilt in 1792. It was known as 'The Theatre
in New Street'.

First published 2008 by Tempus Publishing

Reprinted in 2015 by
The History Press
The Mill, Brimscombe Port
Stroud, Gloucestershire, GL5 2QG
www.thehistorypress.co.uk

British Library Cataloguing in Publication Data.
A catalogue record for this book is available from the British Library.

ISBN 978 0 7524 4660 8

Typesetting and origination by The History Press
Printed in Great Britain

Contents

Acknowledgements

Thanks are due to the following for their assistance in the production of this book: Birmingham Central Library Archives and Heritage, for the use of historical photographs; Alton Douglas, Laurie Hornsby and Sir Derek Jacobi for their photographs and biographical information; Mary Wothers for permission to use photograph of David Hughes and last, but not least, Anthony Spettigue, for the current photographs.

Introduction

William Hutton – Birmingham's first historian – writing in the eighteenth century stated that the earliest theatrical performances in Birmingham were given by groups of strollers. They used a wooden shed in a field, on the site now occupied by Temple Street. By 1740 an actual theatre had been erected in Moor Street, although this was probably no more than an enlarged booth and was not particularly successful. Improvements arrived when a London company arrived, advertised as 'His Majesty's servants from the Theatres Royal in London' – probably more strolling players. This group met with great success and the interest taken by Birmingham residents was so intense that another theatre was erected in King Street. Listed below is information on some of the city's major theatres.

KING STREET THEATRE

The King Street theatre was built in 1752: it was then enlarged in 1774 and the Moor Street building closed. This building was the 'cast-off theatre' referred to by William Hutton, having been procured by the Methodists in 1764, and used by them until 1782. It is probable that New Street Station now occupies the site, although some local historians claim the theatre was actually located in a narrow street once known as 'Queen's Alley', which led on to New Street.

The theatre was initially quite successful and it was here that Mrs Siddons made her first appearance before taking London by storm. In the same year that it was enlarged, it began to face opposition from the brand new theatre in New Street – later to become the Theatre Royal – and in 1779 it closed. The following year it was sold to the Countess of Huntingdon for use as a chapel. It was rebuilt in 1842, but it was demolished a few years later during the New Street station and Queen's Hotel construction.

THEATRE ROYAL

The Theatre Royal, situated in New Street, was built in 1774, and was twice destroyed by fire and rebuilt. In 1780, a superb portico was erected and it was pronounced 'one of the finest theatres in Europe'. At its completion it was known as the 'Theatre in New Street'.

On the morning of 17 August 1792, it was deliberately burnt down. The proprietors offered a reward to bring the criminals to justice, but without success. They rebuilt it, and in 1795 there arose a 'new building which was thought at the time to be of elegance and grandeur not equalled by any in the Provinces'. Macready, the father of the great Charles Macready, was given the job of manager. He was already known as a player and writer, having won great success at Covent Garden, and (what was rare in those days) had saved a great fortune. Under his regime leading players of the day appeared in rapid succession, among whom were Mrs Siddons, her brother, John Philip Kemble, the 'Infant Roscius' (Master W.H. Betty) and Charles Kemble.

On the retirement of the elder Macready in 1813, Robert William Elliston became the lessee, and in 1814 Edmund Kean again appeared in Birmingham, no longer a poor strolling player, but a famous actor, fresh from amazing success in London.

Disaster occurred again in 1820 when the theatre was destroyed by fire after a performance of Sheridan's *Pizarro*. Only the façade remained, but in six months it was rebuilt with a large stage and seating for 2,500 people - it remained unchanged until the beginning of the twentieth century. Prior to 1834, the evening concerts in connection with the Triennial Music Festivals were given in this theatre, and the 1840s saw the success of the first great pantomime, called *Harlequin and the Knight of the Silver Shield, or, The Goblin Mill*. This gave rise to those great Christmas shows that we love today. It was again entirely rebuilt in 1902-4 and when it was closed and demolished in 1956 the building was the fourth 'Theatre Royal' on the site.

REPERTORY THEATRE

This theatre's repertoire was wide and included innovative modern-dress Shakespeare, medieval moralities, Greek drama and modern experimental dramas. Barry Jackson, its creator, was knighted for his services to the theatre in 1925 and along with George Bernard Shaw founded the Malvern Festival in 1929, for which the latter wrote *The Apple Cart*.

Sir Barry Jackson had an excellent eye for young talent and many new actors who later became household names gained valuable early experience with the Rep. In the earlier period Laurence Olivier, Peggy Ashcroft, Edith Evans, Stewart Granger, Margaret Leighton and Ralph Richardson headed the list, while later names included Paul Scofield, Julie Christie, Ian McShane and Derek Jacobi. The 'heart-throb' American actor, Richard Chamberlain, gave a 'bravura' performance as Hamlet in 1969 and lost his soap-opera 'Dr Kildare' tag for ever.

Many plays transferred to London or toured. By 1932 Jackson was supporting four companies and told Shaw that he had spent over £100, 000 supporting the theatre, calling it 'more fun' than running a yacht. However, in spite of the unexpected box office hit *1066 And All That*, finance was a problem, and in 1935 the Birmingham City Council took responsibility for the theatre, founding the Birmingham Repertory Theatre Trust.

From the late 1940s to 1971 various directors took control, including William Armstrong, who came from Liverpool Rep. Douglas Seale staged a famous three-part production of Shakespeare's *Henry VI*, which so influenced the young Peter Dews that he later produced the entire history cycle on BBC television as *An Age of Kings*. Dews was the last director of the Birmingham Repertory Theatre in its original building in Station Street and the first at the new theatre on Broad Street. The new theatre was designed by Graham Winteringham. It opened in 1971 with a performance of *First Impressions*, a musical version of Jane Austen's *Pride and Prejudice* starring Patricia Routledge.

ALEXANDRA THEATRE, JOHN BRIGHT STREET

The architects Owen and Ward combined beauty with elegance, adopting the style of the French Renaissance, for this building. The original façade was surmounted by a figure representing Art, and the interior comprised four comfortable private boxes, a deep pit, pit stalls, dress and upper circles, and gallery. The decorations were in delicately shaded colours of crimson, blue and gold upon a cream ground.

Leon Salberg bought the theatre in 1911 and masterminded the rebuild of the 1930s which gave the 'Alex' its well-known art-deco appearance. Leon Salberg was Polish-born, coming to Britain as a baby (although emigrating to South Africa for a time). He built his reputation as the king of pantomime, producing more than 100 seasonal productions around the country and extending his theatrical empire to include repertory companies in Hereford and at the Grand Theatre, Wolverhampton.

Leon Salberg collapsed and died in his office in 1937 and his son Derek succeeded him, making him Britain's youngest theatre manager at the age of twenty-four. Derek had trained as an accountant before beginning his theatrical career as a stage manager in 1932, becoming general manager at the 'Alex' in 1936.

In the 1970s the board of management decided to drop the resident repertory company and – against Derek's own instincts – the tradition of in-house pantomime productions. Leonard Rossiter, Peggy Mount, John Alderton, Fenella Fielding, Brenda Bruce, Alec McCowan and Arthur Lowe – who himself died suddenly at the 'Alex' – were among the later-to-be famous actors who gained early experience in the Salberg Rep companies. Derek retired in 1977 and died on 29 June 1997, just eleven days before his eighty-fifth birthday. After his retirement, the theatre passed to the control of Birmingham City Council, but then underwent a number of financial difficulties culminating in closure in January 1994 – when a performance of *Pickwick* with Harry Secombe, Roy Castle and Ruth Madoc was cancelled after the city council decided to axe its cash support. However, in April 1994 the theatre was reopened by E & B Production, its new owners. Then, in August 1995, London-based Apollo Theatres – Europe's largest theatre group – bought a twenty-year lease for the building.

This book is not a comprehensive history of theatres and entertainment, but an illustrative account of those buildings and institutions, most of which (but not all) are remembered with affection by 'Brummies' today.

The group of entertainers shown in the text is obviously just a minute sample of the many famous and very talented 'artistes' who have had important connections with Birmingham. These range from Tony Hancock to Sid Field; Kenneth Horne to Ken Tynan; Duran Duran to Wizzard; ELO and the ubiquitous Ozzy Osbourne; Dave Willetts to John Curry and Anne Heywood to Julie Walters. It would take another complete volume to show and list the local 'entertainers' involved in all aspects of show business. Although Michael Balcon is included, information on Birmingham Cinemas is not. This can be found in another publication published by the same group, *Birmingham Cinemas* by Christine Wilkinson and Margaret Hanson.

one

Theatre Royal

For the Benefit of Mr. DIAMOND.

At the THEATRE in NEW-STREET,
This prefent Wednefday Auguft 17th, 1774.
Will be performed A CONCERT of MUSIC.
Boxes Three Shillings, Pit Two Shillings, Gallery One Shilling.
The Doors to be opened at Six, and begin exactly at Seven o'Clock.

Between the feveral Parts of the Concert will be prefented (Gratis)
By a Company of their MAJESTY's Comedians from the Theatres in London-
A COMEDY (not acted thefe Four Years) called

The Conftant Couple;

Or, A TRIP to the JUBILEE.

Sir Harry Wildair by Mr DIAMOND
Beau Clincher by Mr WALDRON
Clincher Jun. by Mr DIDIER
Smuggler by Mr BROOKES
Vizard by Mr ROWSWELL
Dicky by Mr PENN
Tom Errand by Mr GASTRILL
Col. Standard by Mr FARREN
Lady Darling by Mrs DAVIES   Parly by Mrs HUNT
Angelica by Mifs HAMILTON
Lady Lurewell by Mrs DIDIER

End of Act III. A Dance called *The Milliner*, to which will be introduced the
Allemande, by Mr and Mifs WEST.
End of the Play, A New Dance called *Hearts of Oak*, by Mr and Mifs WEST.
To which will be added, A FARCE of Three Acts called

Catherine and Petruchio.

Petruchio by Mr. DIDIER
Baptifta by Mr GASTRILL
Biondello by Mr PITT
Pedro by Mr. PENN

A playbill advertising the first performance at the 'Theatre in New Street', dated Wednesday 17 August 1774.

FEBRUARY 17, 1777.

To the Gentlemen, Clergy, and Inhabitants in General, of the

Town of BIRMINGHAM.

A PETITION having been lately prefented to the Honourable Houfe of Commons for Leave to prefent a Bill to licence a THEATRE lately erected in New-Street, in the faid Town ; and a Petition having fince been prefented, praying that fuch Bill may not pafs into a Law, owing, as it is apprehended, to a Mifreprefentation of the Intention of the Proprietors of faid intended THEATRE; they think it a Duty incumbent upon them to explain to the Public the Motives upon which they have grounded their prefent Application.

Firft, They beg Leave to ftate to the Public, that in their Opinion a PUBLIC THEATRE cannot (if conducted with Propriety) be productive of any ill Confequences to the Town; but on the contrary will afford to the Inhabitants, as well as to the Neighbourhood, an Opportunity of occafional Amufement, founded upon rational and advantageous Principles.

Secondly, The Patent, if obtained, is meant to be vefted in the Proprietors of the THEATRE at Large, and not in the original Petitioner as an Individual.

Thirdly, The Reftrictions inferted in the GAZETTE of To-day, the Proprietors are not only willing, but defirous to fubmit to; or any other that the Public may think expedient and reafonable to recommend.

Fourthly, With Refpect to an Oppofition to the Bill, as originating from the Proprietors of the King-Street Theatre, they flatter themfelves, that they fhall be able not only to fatisfy the Honourable Houfe of Commons, but the whole Town and Neighbourhood, that the Proprietors of fuch latter THEATRE are without the leaft Pretenfion to an Oppofition ; and that the Means made ufe of to fill that Theatre laft Seafon, were (and muft remain till put a Stop to) productive of Mifchiefs and Inconveniences, that the licenfing of the prefent Theatre only can remove.

A broadside detailing reasons for a petition being presented to Parliament to legalise the theatre in Birmingham. Up until 1807, all theatre in Birmingham was strictly illegal. However, it was obvious that the people of the town resented this illegal status, so in 1777 a petition was presented to Parliament in the hope that they would agree to license the new establishment and this broadside gives reasons why the licence should be issued. However, the petition was rejected by a majority of fifty-one – but the theatre continued its business. Following legalisation, the 'Theatre in New Street' changed its name to 'The Theatre Royal'.

The interior of the Theatre Royal in the 1840s. This was the third building on the site of the original, dating from 1820 – the first two were both destroyed by fire.

On occasions the Theatre Royal was used for formal dances or 'balls'. This illustrates one which took place around 1846, following a musical entertainment (possibly the Birmingham Triennial Musical Festival), at the Town Hall. According to a contemporary witness: 'The pit was boarded over and formed a fine surface of considerable extent for the dancers. The upper tier of boxes, and also the gallery, were appropriated to persons wishing to enjoy from afar the gay and splendid scene. Both boxes and gallery were crowded almost to suffocation. The ball itself was attended by a numerous and most brilliant assemblage, including all the beauty and fashion of the neighbourhood.'

A typical Theatre Royal playbill advertising the current production on Tuesday 3 October 1848 – *Romeo and Juliet*.

Theatre Royal staff taking a well-earned 'Theatrical Rest', *c.* 1895.

A scenic artist at work at the theatre, 1896.

The ultra-modern electric switch board at the Theatre Royal, 1896.

Looking towards the orchestra pit and the stage, 1896.

New Street showing the Theatre Royal (behind lamp-post on left) and adjacent buildings in November 1901.

The back of the Theatre Royal as viewed from Stephenson Street, 1901.

The coffee room at the Theatre Royal, 1901.

The stage and proscenium from
the dress circle, 1901.

The auditorium from the front of the stage, 1901.

The 'ballet room' at the Theatre Royal, 1901.

The working property room, 1901.

Props waiting to be used, 1901.

A group of masks stored above the dome of the auditorium, 1901.

The 'star' dressing room, 1901. Would any of today's most notable actors and actresses settle for a room like this?

The 'first lead' dressing room, 1901.

The stage door in Stephenson Street and the theatre commissionaire, 1901.

The circle bar, showing that a certain George Bragg held the licence to sell alcohol, 1901.

George Bragg's bar for non-theatrical 'punters' in an area below the theatre, 1901.

George Bragg's wine cellars in the theatre, 1901.

A view of the wine cellar, 1901.

Members of the male staff of the Theatre Royal in the gallery yard around the time of the last performance, January 1902.

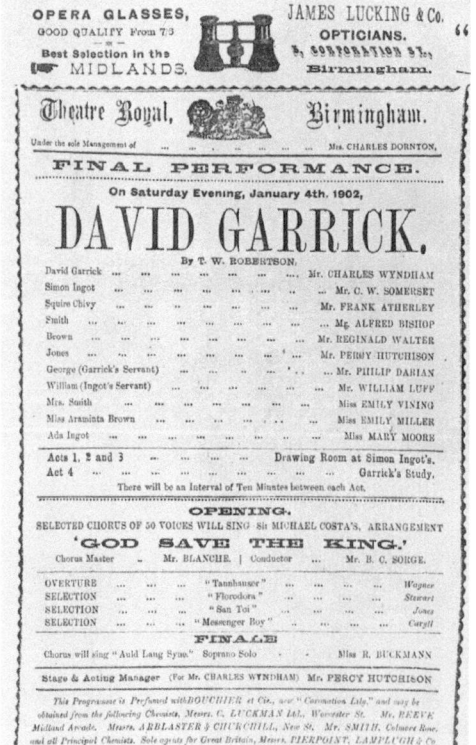

A playbill advertising the final performance at this theatre – *David Garrick* – before it was due to be demolished and rebuilt yet again, 4 January 1902.

A farewell dinner for theatre staff held on the stage after the last performance on 4 January 1902.

The demolition of the Theatre Royal as seen from Bennett's Hill, 1902. The new building was ready for business towards the end of 1904 and opened with a production of *Babes in the Wood*.

The front page of a souvenir programme for a 'special matinee' held at the Theatre Royal on 23 October 1918 on behalf of the lady mayoress's Prisoners of War Fund. This fund provided food for the men of the Royal Warwickshire Regiment, who were prisoners of war in Germany and other enemy countries. At that time its executive committee were responsible for sending food parcels and other necessary items to over 1,500 men at a cost of £1,300 per week. To continue for a further twelve months would cost £60,000. They therefore invited a retired, but famous in her day, American-born actress, Mary Anderson, to star in this performance, which included a selection of classical music and scenes from *Romeo and Juliet* and *Macbeth*.

The programme for the very final show at the Theatre Royal – *The Fol-De-Rols*, December 1956.

The frontage of the Theatre Royal on the night of its final performance on 15 December 1956.

The final performance on 15 December 1956.

Cleaners of the theatre on their last day, December 1956.

The site of the Theatre Royal during demolition, December 1956.

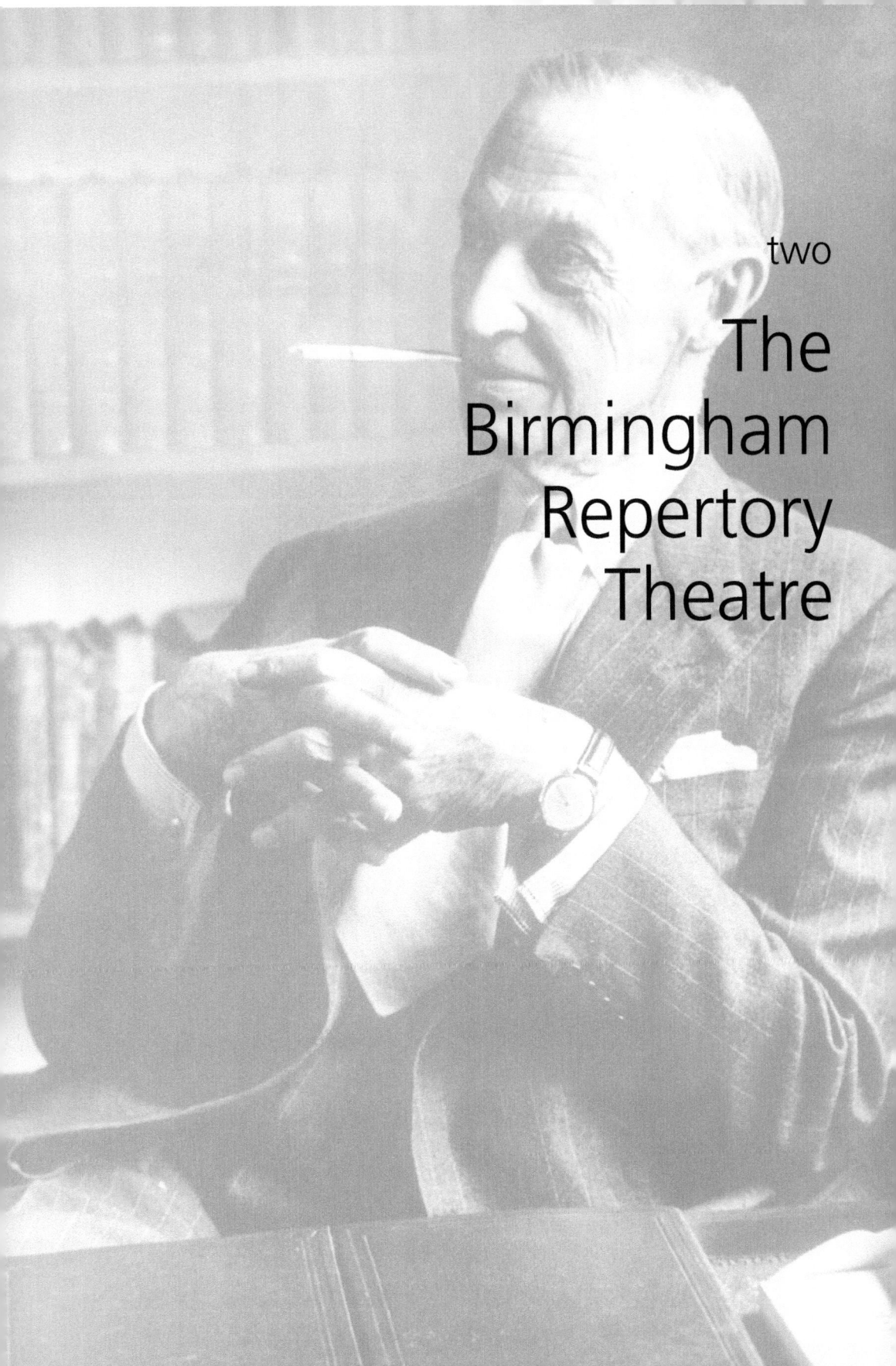

two

The Birmingham Repertory Theatre

Barry Vincent Jackson, founder of the Birmingham Repertory Theatre, as a young man. He was born in Birmingham in 1879, the son of George Jackson, a theatre-loving wealthy merchant who named his son after a favourite actor, Barry Sullivan. Although the young Jackson served his articles as an architect, the theatre proved a stronger attraction and with friends he formed his own amateur company, the Pilgrim Players, who eventually turned professional. On 10 June 1912 the Pilgrim Players announced their plans to build a theatre in Station Street and plans were drawn up under the supervision of the architect, S.N. Cooke. Work began in October and the building was erected in day and night shifts.

The Birmingham Repertory Theatre in its early days. On 15 February 1913, the Birmingham Repertory Theatre opened with a production of Shakespeare's *Twelfth Night* and with Barry Jackson reading the *Lines for the Opening of the Birmingham Repertory Theatre*, written by his friend, poet and playwright John Drinkwater.

EVENINGS AT 7.30.
MATINÉE : THURSDAY AT 2.30.

Quality Street

A Comedy in Four Acts.

By J. M. BARRIE.

Produced by W. G. FAY.

Scenery designed by HUGH OWEN.

Characters in the order of their appearance : —

Miss Fanny Willoughby	Jane Welsh
Miss Willoughby	Margaret Chatwin
Miss Susan	Maud Gill
Miss Henrietta Turnbull	Elana Aherne
Miss Phœbe	Dorothy Turner
Patty	Isabel Thornton
Recruiting Sergeant	Charles Leighton
Valentine Brown	H. Worrall Thompson
Georgy	Marion Dunkley
Arthur Wellesley Thomson	Evelyn Turner
William	Josette Macsherry
Isabella	Nancy McBride
Three Little Girls	Glenys Brett / Marjorie Lord / Joan Shaw
Miss Charlotte Parrat	Hilda Miles
Ensign Blades	Laurence Olivier
Harriet	Kitty Fisher
Lieut. Spicer	Stringer Davis
An Old Soldier	Robert Lang
A Gallant	Howell Davies
Officers	A. L. D'Abreu / F. A. D'Abreu
A Lady	Ida Gilbert

ACT I.   The blue and white Room in the House of the Misses Susan and Phœbe Throssel in Quality Street.

ACT II.   The same room. Ten years later.

ACT III.   The Ball; a canvas pavilion used as retiring room

ACT IV.   The same as Acts I. and II.

Uniforms by Theatricals, Birmingham.

Barry Jackson, knighted in 1925 for services to the theatre, had an excellent eye for young talent, and many young actors who later became world famous gained valuable early experience with The Rep. In the early period these included Peggy Ashcroft, Edith Evans, Stewart Granger, Ralph Richardson and, as this programme from 1927 shows, Laurence Olivier, later Lord Olivier.

One of the popular plays of the 1930s was *The Barretts of Wimpole Street* by Rudolf Besier and here can be seen Elspeth March as Elizabeth Moulton-Barrett and Stephen Murray (later to find fame in BBC radio's comedy series, *The Navy Lark*) as her stern father, Edward Moulton-Barrett, in The Rep's production of October 1935.

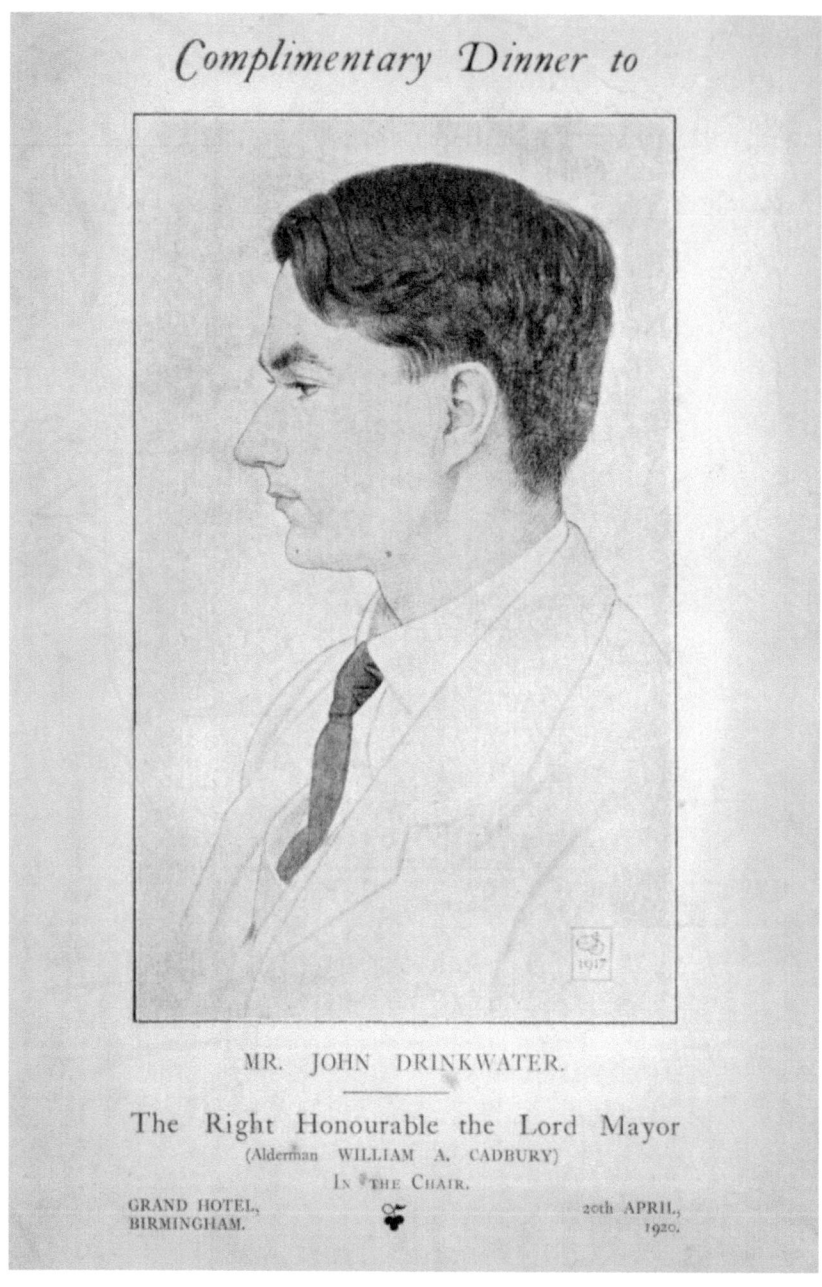

Complimentary Dinner to

MR. JOHN DRINKWATER.

The Right Honourable the Lord Mayor
(Alderman WILLIAM A. CADBURY)
In the Chair.

GRAND HOTEL,
BIRMINGHAM.

20th APRIL,
1920.

John Drinkwater (1882–1937). John started his career in insurance at Nottingham, later transferring to Birmingham. Here he met and became friendly with Barry Jackson, forming the Pilgrim Players with him. He not only acted but wrote and produced plays, and became first producer at the Birmingham Repertory Theatre. One of his plays – *Abraham Lincoln* – moved to London after a successful Birmingham run and proved to be the outstanding feature of the theatrical season of 1918 and 1919. On 20 April 1920 a complimentary dinner was held in his honour at the Grand Hotel, Colmore Row, with the Lord Mayor of Birmingham, Alderman William A. Cadbury presiding, as this copy of the menu shows.

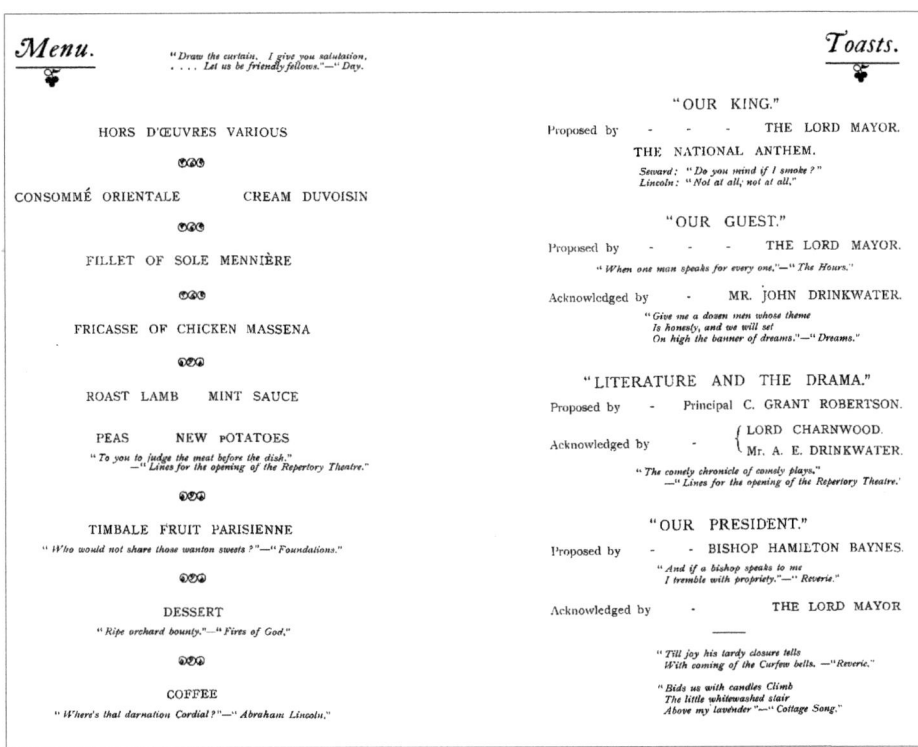

The menu for the dinner held in honour of John Drinkwater.

Repertory celebrities at the Queens Hotel, Stephenson Street. Shown are Sir Hugh Walpole, Sir Barry Jackson, Miss Cecily Byrne, unknown gentleman, Miss Gwen Ffrangcon-Davies, and Mr Ernest Thesiger.

Barry Jackson in his later years. He was to die in April 1961, at the age of eighty-one.

The Rep in its later years.

The box office at The Rep,
c. 1971.

The ropes used to hold sets above the stage at The Rep in Station Street, *c.* 1971.

A sewing machine in the wardrobe room at The Rep, *c.* 1971.

The workshop at The Rep, *c.* 1971.

At work in the wardrobe room, *c.* 1971.

The last performance at Station Street, 3 April 1971.

The original Rep building today – now
known as 'The Old Rep Theatre' and
in continued use by both amateur and
professional actors, especially the Birmingham
Stage Co. Photograph taken in May 2007.
(courtesy of Anthony Spettigue)

The foundation stone of the new Rep was laid by Miss Jennie Lee, Minister for the Arts, on Saturday 25 October 1969. It was designed by Graham Winteringham and opened on its new site in Broad Street two years later, in October 1971. This photograph of the architect's model shows just how modern it would be.

The theatre when almost new in 1971. The colonnade obstructing part of the view was eventually taken down and rebuilt as part of the 'Peace Garden' at St Thomas's church, Bath Row.

A photograph of The Rep, taken from close to the former registry office. It shows the statue of Boulton, Watt and Murdoch, which was later taken down and re-gilded. The photograph dates from around 1980.

The Rep before the building of the International Convention Centre. Part of what was Bingley Hall can be seen to the left. This was partly destroyed by fire in January 1984 and completely demolished in June of the same year.

The Rep showing an extension of offices and suites to the right of the original building and the International Convention Centre (opened in 1991) to the left.

To the right can be seen 'Forward' – a statue by Birmingham-born sculptor, Raymond Mason. Made from fibreglass, it caused much controversy when unveiled in 1991. It was later destroyed when set on fire by a young man.

The Rep showing the 'Spirit of Enterprise' – a fountain acting as an allegory of modern multicultural Birmingham, designed by Tom Lomax and unveiled in 1991.

The Rep today. (courtesy of Anthony Spettigue)

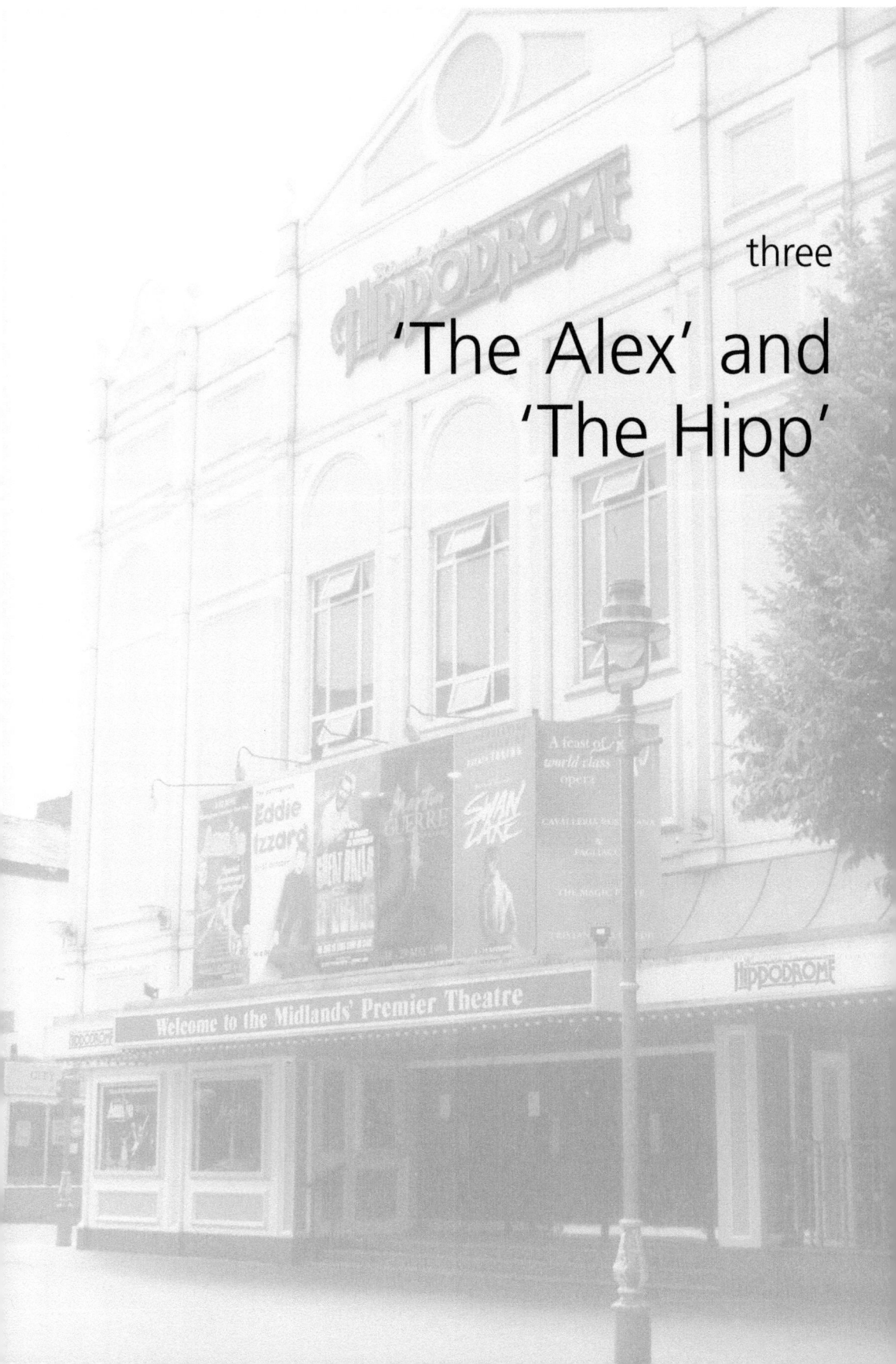

three

'The Alex' and 'The Hipp'

The Alexandra Theatre in John Bright Street, opened in 1901 under the name 'The Lyceum Theatre'. It was owned by William Coutts, who had paid £10,000, and it was capable of seating 2,000 people. The photograph shows the site shortly after it had been secured by Coutts, *c.* 1899. Just over one year after it opened Coutts sold the theatre to Lester Collingwood for just £4,500, the first months of business having been a failure, and in 1902 its name was changed to 'The Alexandra', after the current Queen – wife of Edward VII.

The Alex in 1975. In 1968 it was sold to the city of Birmingham by its then owner, Derek Salberg; the same year saw an extension bridge constructed from the building in John Bright Street to Suffolk Street, making it more obvious to the passer-by, and providing a more prominent frontage with extra space for a box office – an improvement that cost £74,000. The photograph shows this frontage in 1975.

The Suffolk Street frontage today. (courtesy of Anthony Spettigue)

A side view of the current building, showing part of the original façade behind in John Bright Street. (courtesy of Anthony Spettigue)

The Alex's most famous owner/manager, Derek Salberg (on the right), with popular entertainer, Clarkson Rose, with pen; Phyllis Bushill-Matthews, daughter of Philip Rodway, one time manager of the Theatre Royal, and Mrs Salberg. The photograph was taken at the last performance at the Theatre Royal, New Street on 15 December 1956.

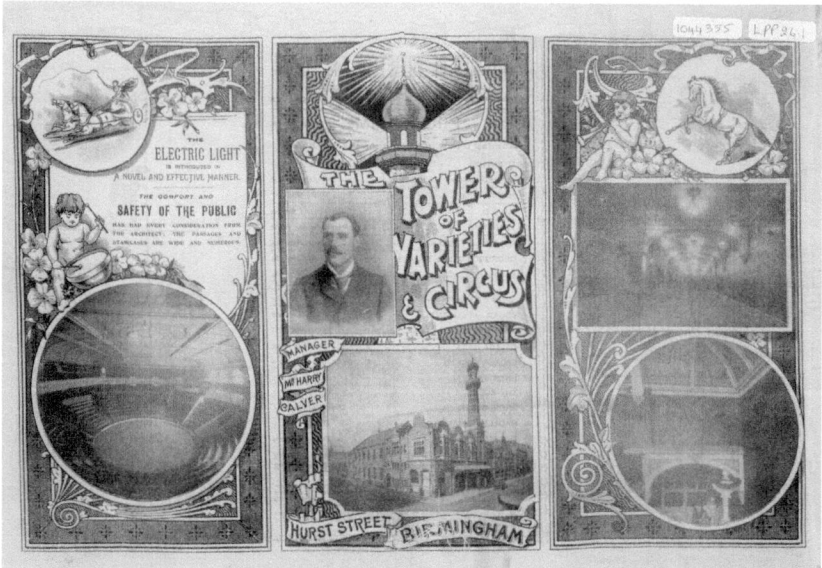

The night of 9 October 1899 saw the opening in Hurst Street of what was to become the Birmingham Hippodrome. However, it did not open as a theatre, but as a circus known as 'The Tower of Varieties and Circus'. It was built by two brothers, James and Henry Draysey. Its prominent tower remained until 1960, when it had to be demolished after becoming unsafe.

THE TOWER OF VARIETIES AND CIRCUS,
HURST STREET, BIRMINGHAM.
General Manager - - - Mr. HARRY CALVER

[ONE PENNY.]   **PROGRAMME.**   [ONE PENNY.]

Monday Oct. 9, 1899, and during the Week.

1—OVERTURE	- -	"Masaniello"	- - - - Auber
2—ALFRED CLARK	- - -	- - -	Juggling Act
3—MARTINETTES	- - -	- - "The Music Master"
4—VALD O	- - -	- - -	Entree
5—YESOKICHI	- - -	- Perpendicular Rope
6 ATLAS and VULCANA	- -	Modern Athletes
7—GEORGE LEGLERE TROUPE	- - -	Acrobats
8—CLIFFE BERZAC	Wrestling and Boxing Pony, also his Wonderful Leaping Boarhound "Pasha"
9—BROS. LEONARD	- - -	- -	Horizontal Bar
10—EDGAR and EUGENE	- - -	Banjoists
11—JOHN FREDERICK CLARK	- -	Somersault Act
12—CELEST	- - -	The Wire King
13—ESCALADORS (3)	-	Double Ladder Balancers
14—BROS. NOEL	- - -	- -	Entrée
15—THE ZOES	- - -	Flying Trapeze
16—BROS. CLARK	- -	Double Jockey Act
17—MADLLE. TAMAMOTO	- -	Sword Walker
18—THE MAYOS	- - -	Funny Skaters
19—WILLIE RICHARDS, alias "Rabbit," will make himself generally useful during the evening
20—GOD SAVE THE QUEEN.

Equestrian Director and Ring Master - - - Mr. R. ROBERTS
Musical Director - - - - - - Mr. E. DAVIS

NOTICE—For the benefit of the Public we beg to state that the Performance will commence every night at 7-30 punctu, and terminate at 10-30 to the minute, so as to enable visitors from the surrounding districts to get home before 11 o'clock.

JAMES UPTON, Printer, Cambridge Street, Birmingham.

GRAND

OPENING · NIGHT,

MONDAY, OCTOBER 9th, 1899.

GRAND

OPENING · NIGHT,

MONDAY, OCTOBER 9th, 1899.

The programme for the first night.

The original auditorium could hold 3,000 and it also had a proscenium and a stage as well as a circus ring. However, the circus flopped and closed within five weeks. Under the guidance of its original architect, F.W. Lloyd, the building was reconstructed, its capacity cut to 1,900 and its name changed to 'The Tivoli'. It opened on 20 August 1900 as a variety hall and its name changed to the Birmingham Hippodrome in 1903. The photograph shows a newsvendor in Victoria Square in February 1902 advertising a story that related to the death of an artisté at The Tivoli.

Left: A programme dating from the early years of the theatre as the 'Hippodrome', 1906.

Below: In 1979 the Birmingham City Council bought the theatre for £50,000 and leased it to a non-profitable charitable organisation known as The Birmingham Hippodrome Theatre Trust Ltd. Major alterations were then made throughout 1981 and it reopened with a production of *Jesus Christ Superstar.*

Much improvement was carried out in the following years and construction of a new frontage was carried out in 1986. This photograph shows the frontage in 1999.

The Birmingham Hippodrome closed on 29 January 2000 – two months after The Royal Variety Performance had been held there in the presence of the Queen – to continue work on a £28.5 million Hippodrome 2000 Development Project – a partnership between The Birmingham Hippodrome, Birmingham Royal Ballet and DanceXchange, supported by The National Lottery through the Arts Council of England, Birmingham City Council, the European Development Fund and donations from the public. It reopened in November 2001, a little later than expected, but to much acclaim. This photograph, taken in May 2007, shows the great changes to the frontage. (courtesy of Anthony Spettigue)

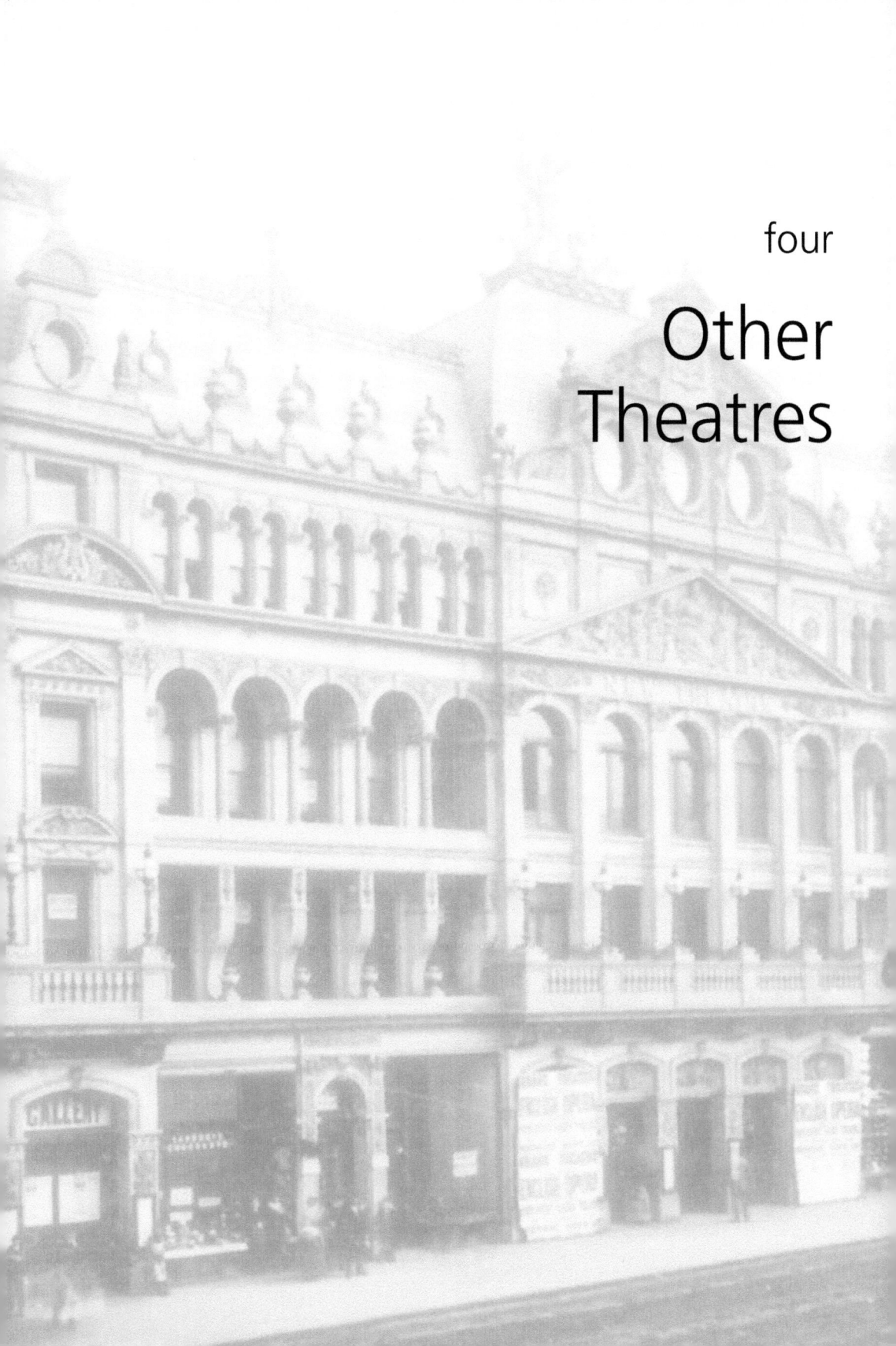

four

Other
Theatres

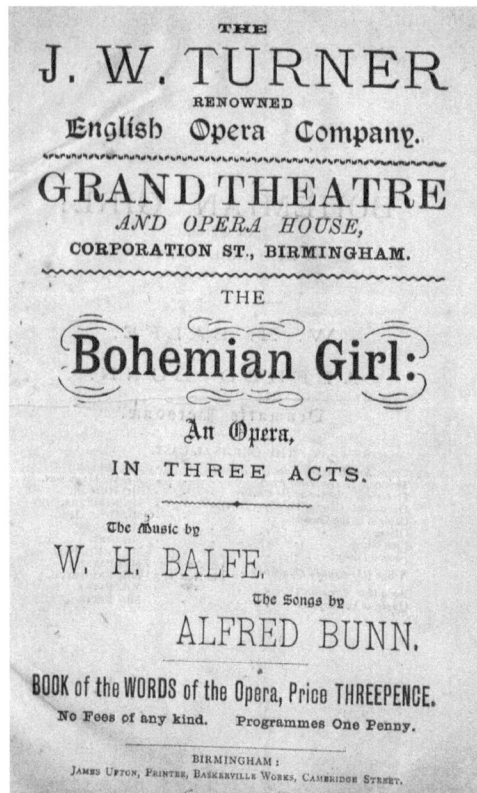

Above: The Grand Theatre, Corporation Street, *c.* 1890. It opened in 1883 and was situated on the corner of Corporation Street and James Watt Street. Designed by W.H. Ward, and built by Bradney & Co., a local firm, it was the largest theatre in the city, seating 2,200. Intended to be called the New Theatre, 'Grand' had been added by its opening day and the 'New' dropped soon afterwards. Frank Matcham, was engaged to redesign the interior by its new owner, Moss Empires, who turned it into a music hall – 'The Grand Theatre of Varieties'.

Left: The front page of the programme for an extremely successful and popular opera in its day, *The Bohemian Girl* (with music by W.H. Balfe and the lyrics by Alfred Bunn), which was performed at the Grand Theatre in 1888. Note the cost of the programme and for a little extra you could purchase *The Book of the Words of the Opera.*

Souvenir of
Miss Vesta Tilley's
Farewell Visit
to
Birmingham
and of her association with
the New Crippled Children's
Convalescent Home

Grand Theatre, Birmingham
December, 1919

As a music hall, The Grand attracted household names like George Robey, W.C. Fields, Marie Lloyd and Birmingham's own 'matinee idol', Vesta Tilley. Vesta chose to appear at The Grand in her farewell visit to Birmingham in December 1919 and to make it a charitable event, with proceeds going to the new Convalescent Home for Birmingham's Crippled Children, near Tanworth-in-Arden, Warwickshire. This photograph of the programme for the event shows Vesta in her stage clothes.

Vesta Tilley as herself with her dogs.

Another household name to appear at The Grand was Sir Harry Lauder, and on 8 March 1926 the Rotary Clubs of R.I.B.I. (Rotary International of Britain and Ireland) organised a Rotary Night, held in his honour as a rotarian, at The Grand.

Victoria Palace Theatre
London.

The Rotary Spirit surely is in dear old Birmingham, let us hope Friendship may rule the world. Happy we'll be a' th'gither.

Harry Lauder

A message from Sir Harry Lauder at the time of the Rotary Night held in his honour.

The Prince of Wales Theatre, Broad Street. The building was erected as a music hall in 1856 and was intended for high-class concerts, not variety, but in 1862 it became licensed as a theatre as 'The Royal Music Hall Operetta House'. In the following year it became 'The Prince of Wales Operetta House', and shortly afterwards 'The Prince of Wales Theatre'. In 1876 it was entirely reconstructed and a new façade added. It became very successful and five years later was almost completely rebuilt.

A poster for a play starring popular actress Sybil Thorndike in 1929. In 1918, Philip Rodway, manager of the Theatre Royal, persuaded his company to buy the shares of The Prince of Wales Birmingham Ltd, and the two theatres then came under one management with Rodway in control, only moving to The Prince of Wales when the Theatre Royal was sold in 1929. Under his regime The Prince of Wales catered for all with productions ranging from opera, ballet, Shakespeare, to Shaw, comedies and musicals.

Prince of Wales auditorium. On 9 April 1941, when the Anglo-Polish Ballet Co. were the attraction, the theatre suffered a direct hit by German bombers and its interior was completely obliterated. The remaining shell of the building was demolished in 1947.

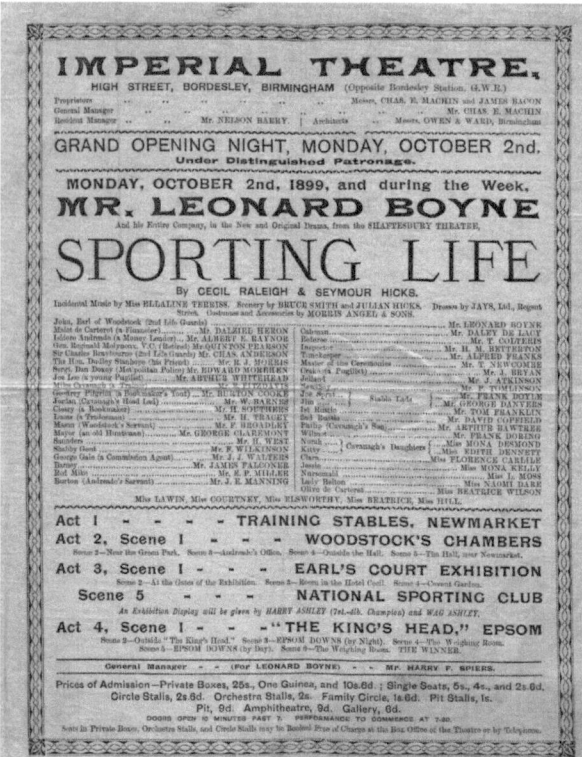

The Imperial Theatre, later Bordesley Palace, opened on 2 October 1899 as 'The Imperial', where popular dramas acted by the best touring companies were played at popular prices. Messrs Owen and Ward, the architects, displayed excellent taste in construction and decoration. The interior was so arranged that an uninterrupted view was obtained from all parts. The photograph shows the programme for the opening night.

The Imperial closed on 25 April 1903, reopening again in August of that year as a music hall under the name 'Bordesley Palace' and continued as such until December 1907, when it was again licensed for stage plays. It closed as a theatre on 29 December 1928, became a cinema in 1929 and closed down in 1942.

Aston Hippodrome just before it was demolished in 1980. It opened on 7 December 1908 after being built at a cost of £10,000. It was designed by James Lister & Co., who had also designed the Barton's Arms public house in the same area – there is a story that as a young man, Charlie Chaplin played at the Aston Hipp and spent his spare time in the Barton's Arms. In 1938 the theatre was seriously damaged by a fire which resulted in refurbishment costing £38,000. Among the famous acts which appeared here were Laurel and Hardy, George Formby and Gracie Fields.

On 4 June 1960, the theatre gave its final performance – a revue entitled *A to Z of Striptease* – the type of show which dominated its stage from the mid to late 1950s. It was then turned into a bingo hall and remained so until its demolition in September 1980, which this photograph shows.

The Drum – a centre dedicated to developing and promoting contemporary art and culture of British African, Asian and Caribbean communities – now stands on the site of the Aston Hippodrome. (courtesy of Anthony Spettigue)

The Empire Theatre opened on 7 May 1894 as 'The New Empire Palace of
Varieties'. Advertised as 'The Most Beautiful Variety Theatre in England', it was
designed by the theatre architect Frank Matcham. It stood on the corner of
Smallbrook Street and Hurst Street and occupied the site on which Day's Crystal
Palace Concert Hall had stood, which in turn occupied the site of the White Swan
Public House before it was turned to a place of musical entertainment by owner
James Day. The Concert Hall was in business from 1862 to 1893. The photograph
shows The Empire in 1912.

An interior view of The Empire, 1912.

BIRMINGHAM EMPIRE PALACE.

Architect, Mr. FRANK MATCHAM.

Proprietors - - - The BIRMINGHAM EMPIRE PALACE, Ltd.
Managing Director - - - - - - Mr. H. E. MOSS
General Manager - - - - - - Mr. FRANK ALLEN

✢ PROGRAMME. ✣

GRAND OPENING NIGHT,
MONDAY, MAY 7th, 1894.

The Entertainment will commence at 7-30 by Miss LUCY CLARKE singing the National Anthem.

1—OVERTURE - "Die Felsenmuhle" - - *Reissiger*
2—J. H. HURST - - Character Comedian and Mimic
3—LENTON FAMILY - - Drawing-room Entertainment
4—Mr. and Mrs. LUCAS - - - Musical Sketch Artistes
5—WAL PINK & Co. - - - Sketch, "The Parrot"
6—BEN NATHAN - - - - - Comedian
7—GUS ELEN - - - - Coster Comedian
8—GRAND SELECTION from Gounod's Opera, "FAUST"
9—F. W. MILLIS - - - - - Ventriloquist
10—LUCY CLARKE - - - - Contralto Vocalist
11—CHIRGWIN - - The White-Eyed Musical Kaffir
12—TILLER SIXTETTE - - Vocalists and Dancers
13—TWO MACS - - Knockabout Comedians
14—ESME and LEON - - Novel Gymnastic Act

On account of the great length of the programme the public are respectfully requested not to indulge in indiscriminate encores, otherwise part of it must necessarily be omitted.

- - - - - - - - - Mr. JOHN SHAW
Acting Manager
Stage Manager - Mr. P. A. LENNON | Musical Director, Mr. ARTHUR GRIMMETT

Left: A programme for the opening night of The Empire, 7 May 1894, which included the popular comedian, Gus Elen.

Below: The Gaiety Theatre of Varieties in Coleshill Street dates from June 1846, when Holders Hotel and Concert Hall was opened, under the proprietor Henry Holder, who ran the Rodney Inn, next door. It was taken over by a number of people through the years and eventually became 'The Birmingham Concert Hall' in the 1870s.

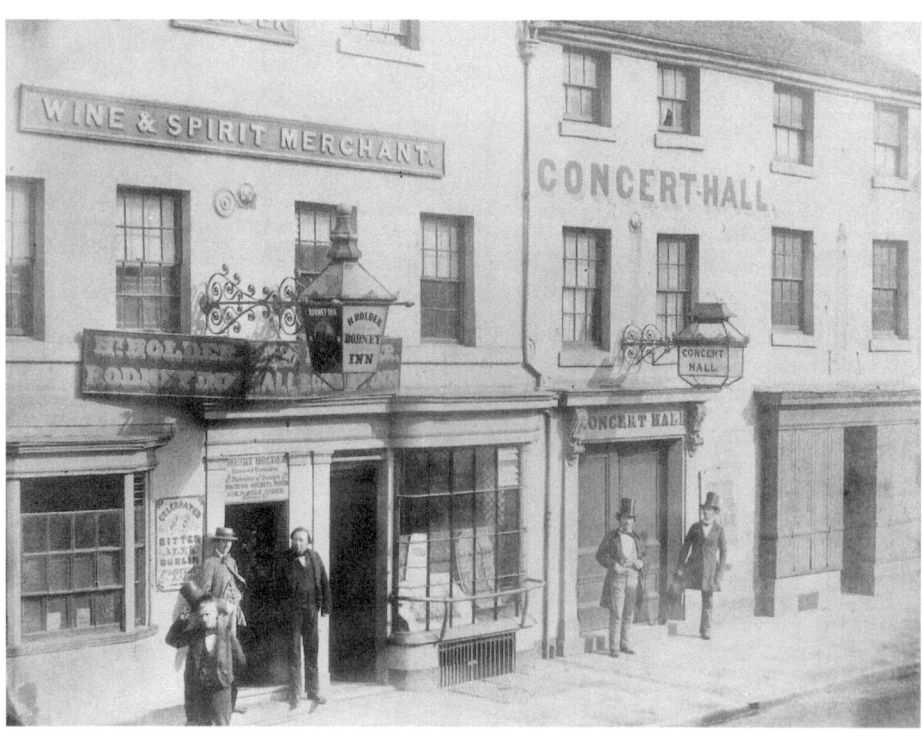

In 1886, after Charles Barnard became the proprietor of the theatre, he changed the name to 'The Gaiety Concert Hall'. By 1896 it was being run by the Gaiety Trust and in 1897 changed to 'The Gaiety Theatre of Varieties'. In the week beginning 7 March 1910, Miss Dorothy Ward – the Birmingham-born entertainer who was later to make her name as a great 'principal boy' in pantomime – was the main attraction, as this poster shows.

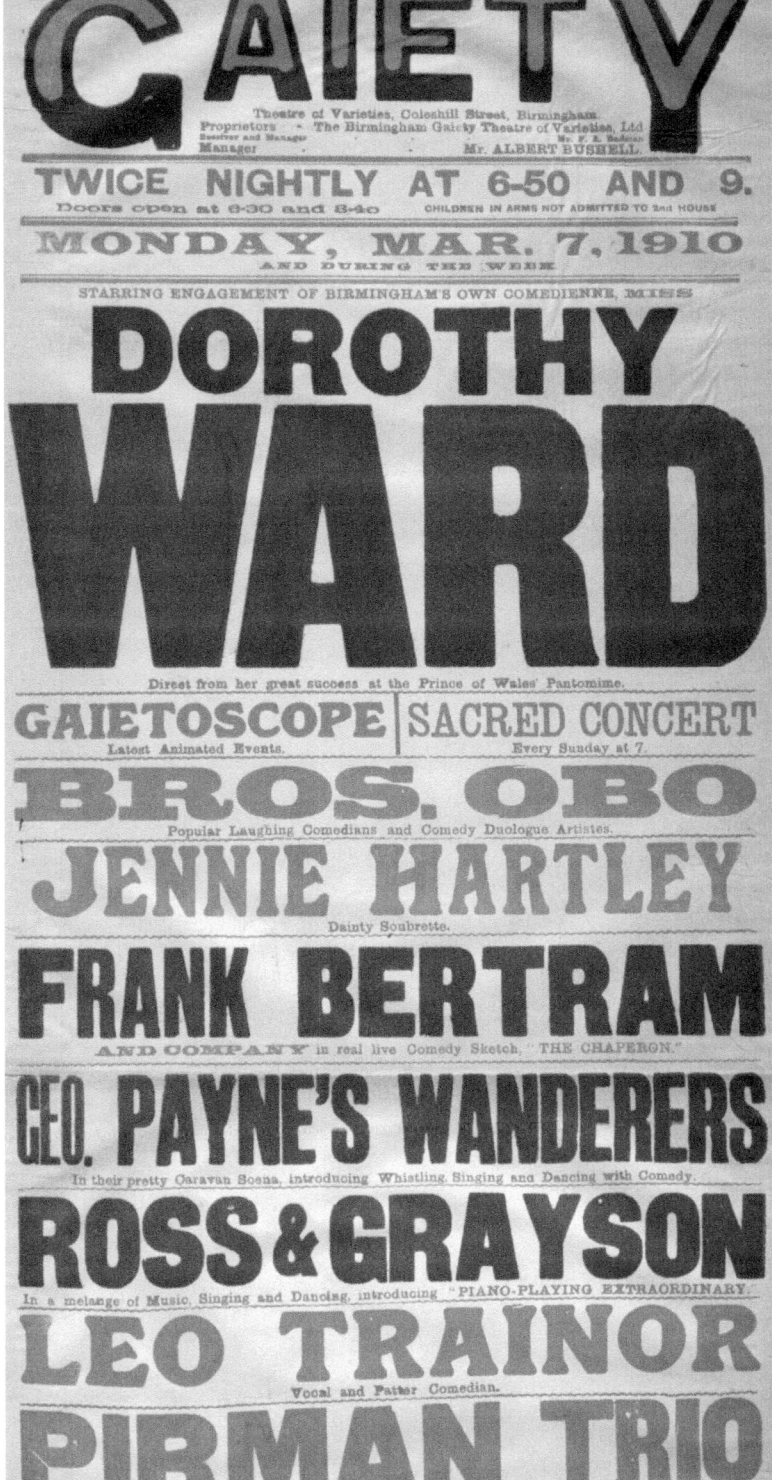

An interior view of the Rodney Inn.

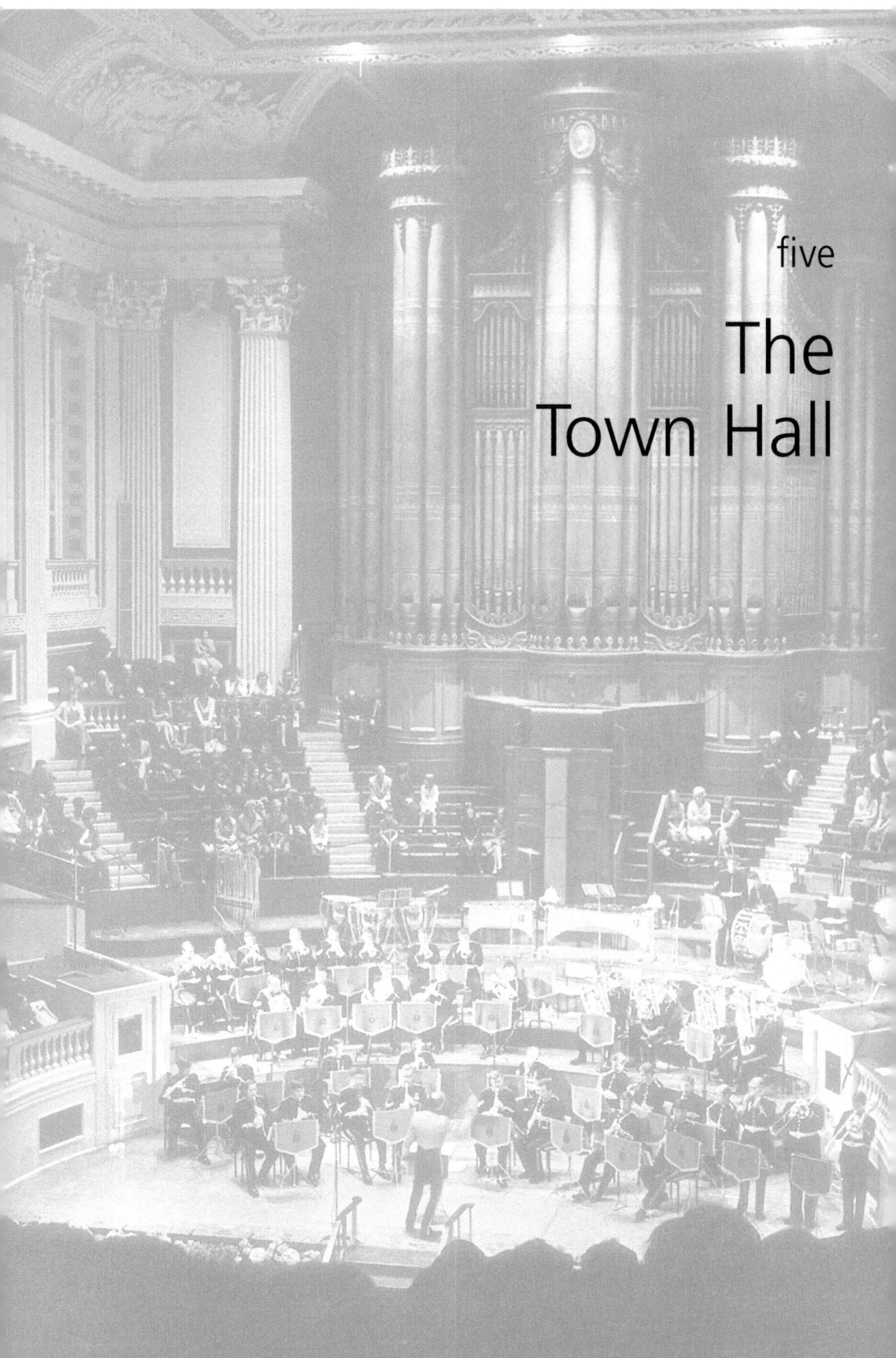

five

The
Town Hall

Birmingham Town Hall, Paradise Street was designed by Joseph Hansom and John Welch and built to house the Birmingham Triennial Musical Festivals and other meetings and events where a large audience was expected.

The Town Hall was built thanks to the effort of Joseph Moore, a partner in a successful firm of button makers and a personal friend of Matthew Boulton and James Watt. From 1802 he took the lead in organising the musical festivals which had continued since 1768 – he engaged the performers, selected the music, chose the 'band' and formed the chorus. Through a petition drawn up in 1827, Moore persuaded the Birmingham Street Commissioners that a building such as a Town Hall was needed and subsequently an architectural competition was put in place.

The Town Hall eventually opened in 1834 and became well-known through the powerful organ towering over the scene as you entered the building. For the opening events every space was taken and hundreds of disappointed people were turned away.

In 1846 the great German composer, Felix Mendelssohn, returned to Birmingham – he had previously taken part in the 1837 and 1840 festivals – to conduct the premiere of his immortal *Elijah*. Mendelssohn also had another artistic side to him as this sketch, showing his vision of Birmingham, shows.

THE GRAND ORGAN IN THE TOWN HALL BIRMINGHAM.

The Town Hall organ, always the focal point of the hall, was built by William Hill and completely rebuilt between 1982 and 1984, being reinstalled in time for the 150th anniversary of the hall, which was celebrated on 6 October 1984.

Over the years many pieces of music, now world famous, were premiered or had their first British performance at the Town Hall, including Antonin Dvorak's *The Spectre's Bride* and Charles Gounod's *Mors et Vita* (both in 1885), Edward Elgar's *Dream of Gerontius* in 1900 and *The Music-Makers* in 1912. This photograph shows the orchestra and choir taking part in the 1876 festival.

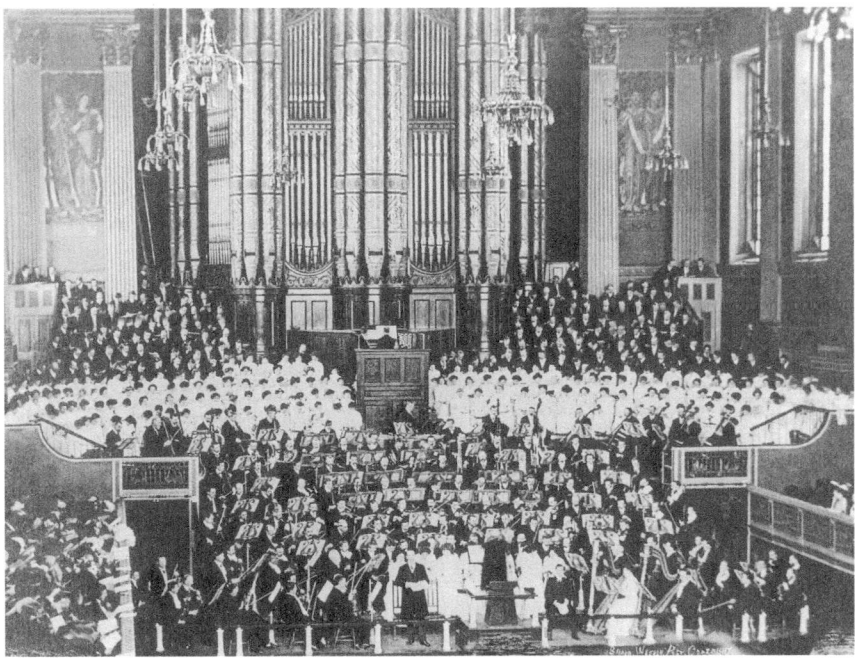

Another musical festival, this time in 1909.

A concert held in the Town Hall in 1917 with the legendary Thomas Beecham as conductor and Neville Chamberlain standing to his left.

Members of the City of Birmingham Symphony Orchestra 'living it up' on the Last Night of the Proms in 1974.

The band of the Royal Marines at the Town Hall in 1975.

The Town Hall organ after refurbishment in the 1980s.

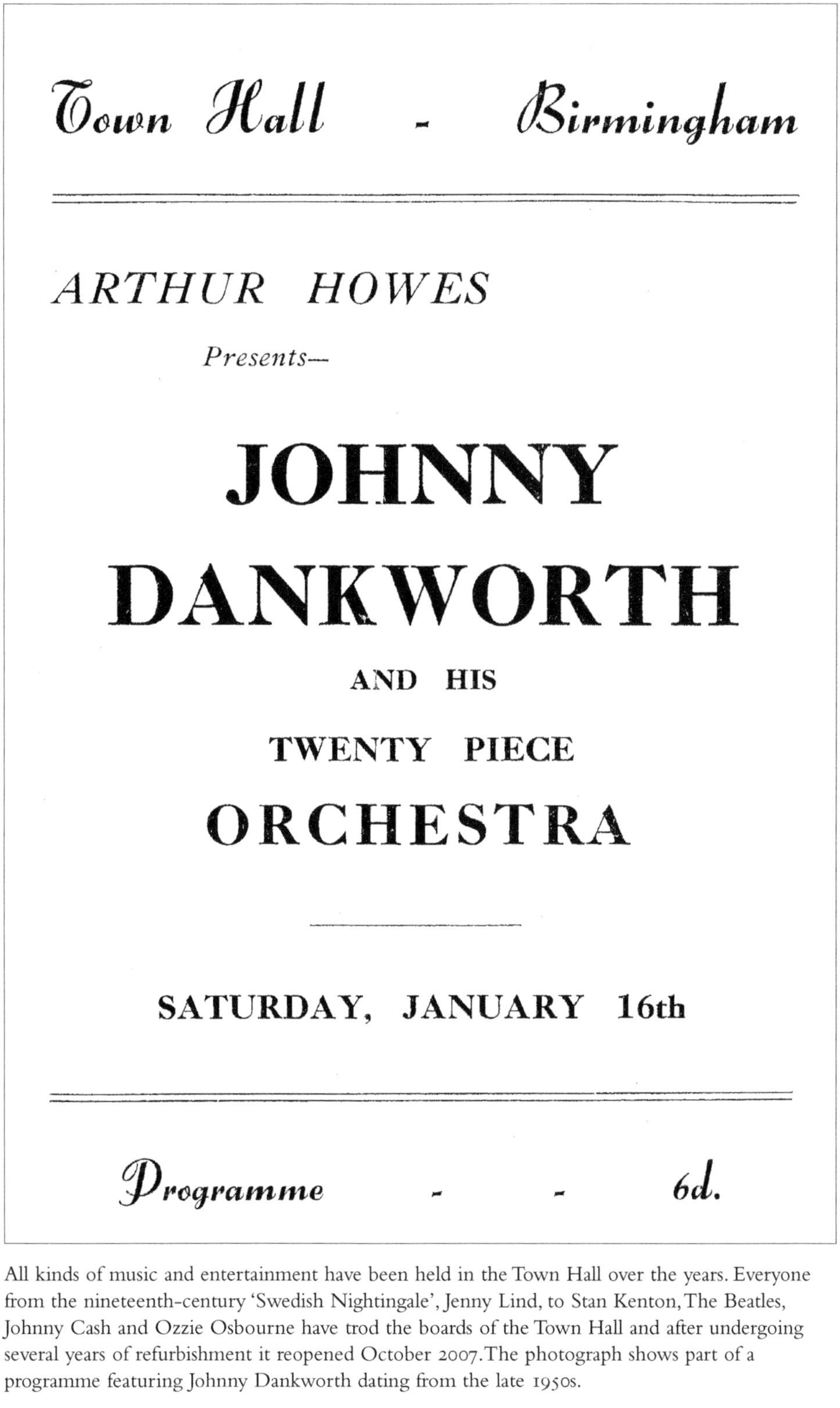

Town Hall - Birmingham

ARTHUR HOWES

Presents—

JOHNNY

DANKWORTH

AND HIS

TWENTY PIECE

ORCHESTRA

SATURDAY, JANUARY 16th

Programme - - *6d.*

All kinds of music and entertainment have been held in the Town Hall over the years. Everyone from the nineteenth-century 'Swedish Nightingale', Jenny Lind, to Stan Kenton, The Beatles, Johnny Cash and Ozzie Osbourne have trod the boards of the Town Hall and after undergoing several years of refurbishment it reopened October 2007. The photograph shows part of a programme featuring Johnny Dankworth dating from the late 1950s.

HAROLD HOLT LTD.
PRESENT

PAUL
ROBESON

SOUVENIR PROGRAMME
PRICE · TWO SHILLINGS

Programme for a Paul Robeson concert. This performance by one of the most charismatic actors and singers of the twentieth century was held in the Town Hall on 25 November 1958.

six

Bingley
Hall

Bingley House – the site for Bingley Hall, Broad Street. This had been built in the 1760s, and from the beginning of the nineteenth century had been home to an important branch of the Lloyd family, Birmingham's first bankers and founders of 'The Black Horse', Lloyds/TSB.

BINGLEY EXHIBITION HALL,
Broad Street, Birmingham.
ERECTED MDCCCL.
Width within the Walls 212 feet._Depth 224 feet.

In 1849, a new society – the Birmingham & Midland Counties Agricultural Association – held a show of cattle, sheep and pigs in a large shed in Lower Essex Street. Its success encouraged them to try again the following year. The only area large enough they found was a plot of land that had recently become vacant after the demolition of Bingley House. The land was owned by the Birmingham Free School (King Edward's) and the society managed to lease the land as well as having an appropriate building constructed, which was to become Bingley Hall. The print shows Bingley Hall when first constructed and is an engraving by Thomas Underwood.

Above and below: The first cattle show held at Bingley Hall in December 1850 as seen in *The Illustrated London News* of 14 December 1850.

CHRISTIAN'S PATE-DE-LICHEN

OR ICELAND MOSS JUJUBES.

During the Winter Months always carry a Box of

THE NATIONAL JUBILEE EXHIBITION
OF
Sporting & Other Dogs
BINGLEY HALL, BIRMINGHAM.

President:
THE EARL OF PLYMOUTH.

Vice-President:
THE RIGHT HON. THE LORD MAYOR OF BIRMINGHAM
(MR. ALDERMAN G. H. KENRICK).

THE WELSH TERRIER "CHAMPION BRYNHIR BALLAD."
Winner of the Challenge Prize and Brewers' Challenge Cup,
National Dog Show and about 40 other Challenge Prizes.
The Property of Mr. Walter S. Glynn.

27th, 28th, 29th January, 1909.

Contents of Catalogue,   Order of Judging,
page 7.   pp. 30 & 31.

HUDSON & SON, Printers, Edmund St. & Livery St., Birm.

For Sore Throats, Hoarseness, Coughs, Colds, &c.

THE INVALUABLE REMEDY

Sole Proprietors: **T. & W. & W. SOUTHALL,**
Pharmaceutical Chemists, 17 Bull St., Birmingham.

Left: Livestock shows continued, as did other shows – including the National Dog Show, miscellaneous industrial exhibitions and the famous Ideal Homes exhibitions. Pat Collins put on his Christmas Circus Show here for a number of years and the British Theatre Exhibition was presented here from 23 May to 18 June 1949, organised by the *Birmingham Post*, Sir Barry Jackson and the Arts Council of Great Britain.

Below: Alcohol was advertised at an exhibition in Bingley Hall in 1893.

Bingley Hall at the time of the Caravan, Camping & Leisure Exhibition in 1981. The site is now occupied by the International Convention Centre.

Bingley Hall was seriously damaged by fire in January 1984, yet the International Custom & Sports Car Show was held there in April of that year. However, this was the last exhibition held there and it was completely demolished in June, as this and the next photograph show.

The demolition of Bingley Hall in June 1984. Symphony Hall and the International Convention Centre were later built on the site and opened in June 1991.

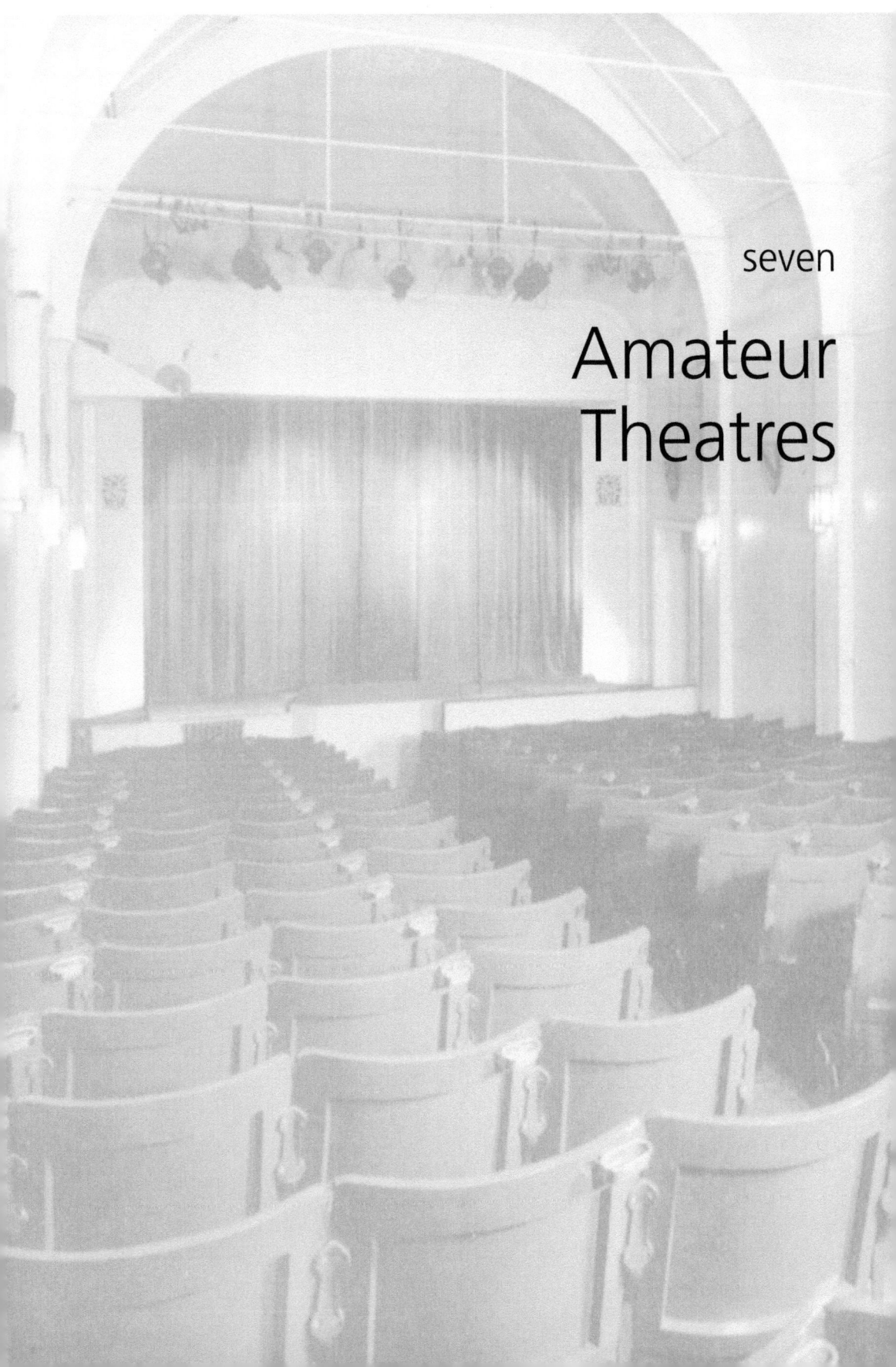

seven

Amateur Theatres

The Crescent Theatre, founded in 1931, originally comprised of amateur theatrical enthusiasts called the Municipal Players, which consisted of city council employees and teachers who had been producing plays in the Council House canteen and the Midland Institute since 1924. They leased three properties on the corner of Cambridge Street and The Crescent (No. 18) and although it was intended to staff the theatre from the public services, this was found to be impractical and anyone with a degree of enthusiasm could join. The theatre was officially opened on 8 April 1932 with a play called *The Romantics* by Edmond Rostand. The photograph shows the auditorium of this tiny theatre, which seated 188 people.

In October 1964 the Crescent Theatre moved into new premises in Cumberland Street. Although an amateur theatre, this was another theatre in Birmingham where, over the years, several well-known actors and performers gained early experience, including Martin Shaw, Anton Lesser and Ruby Turner.

In the late 1980s buildings in Cumberland Street were required to be demolished as the area was to form part of what was to become the showpiece area of Brindley Place. A new building eventually opened in Sheepcote Street in October 1998. This photograph was taken in May 2007. (courtesy of Anthony Spettigue)

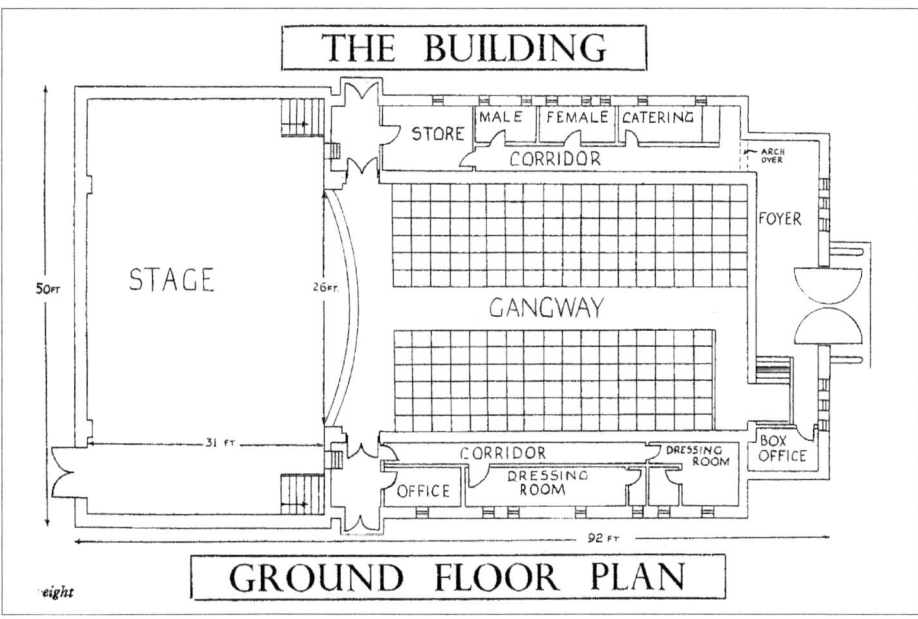

On 1 April 1950, a group of youthful drama enthusiasts took possession of a rubbish dump in Pemberley Road, Acocks Green. They cleared the site and began to dig. One year and one week later on 6 April 1951, they opened the doors to 'The Hall Green Little Theatre' – the ground floor plan of which is shown.

The theatre was enlarged in 1981 with the opening of the Signature Theatre and bar on 30 March by Derek Salberg, CBE, JP, and the photograph shows the theatre today. (courtesy of Anthony Spettigue)

Another local theatre built through the enthusiasm of amateurs is the Highbury Little Theatre at Sheffield Road, Sutton Coldfield. The story began in 1924 when a group known as 'The Highbury Players' held their first meeting. Plays were performed in houses in Erdington and their own theatre – built by voluntary labour – opened in June 1942, as a private members' theatre. Membership was open to members of the public from 1946-7. The photograph shows Highbury Little Theatre in May 2007. (courtesy of Antony Spettigue)

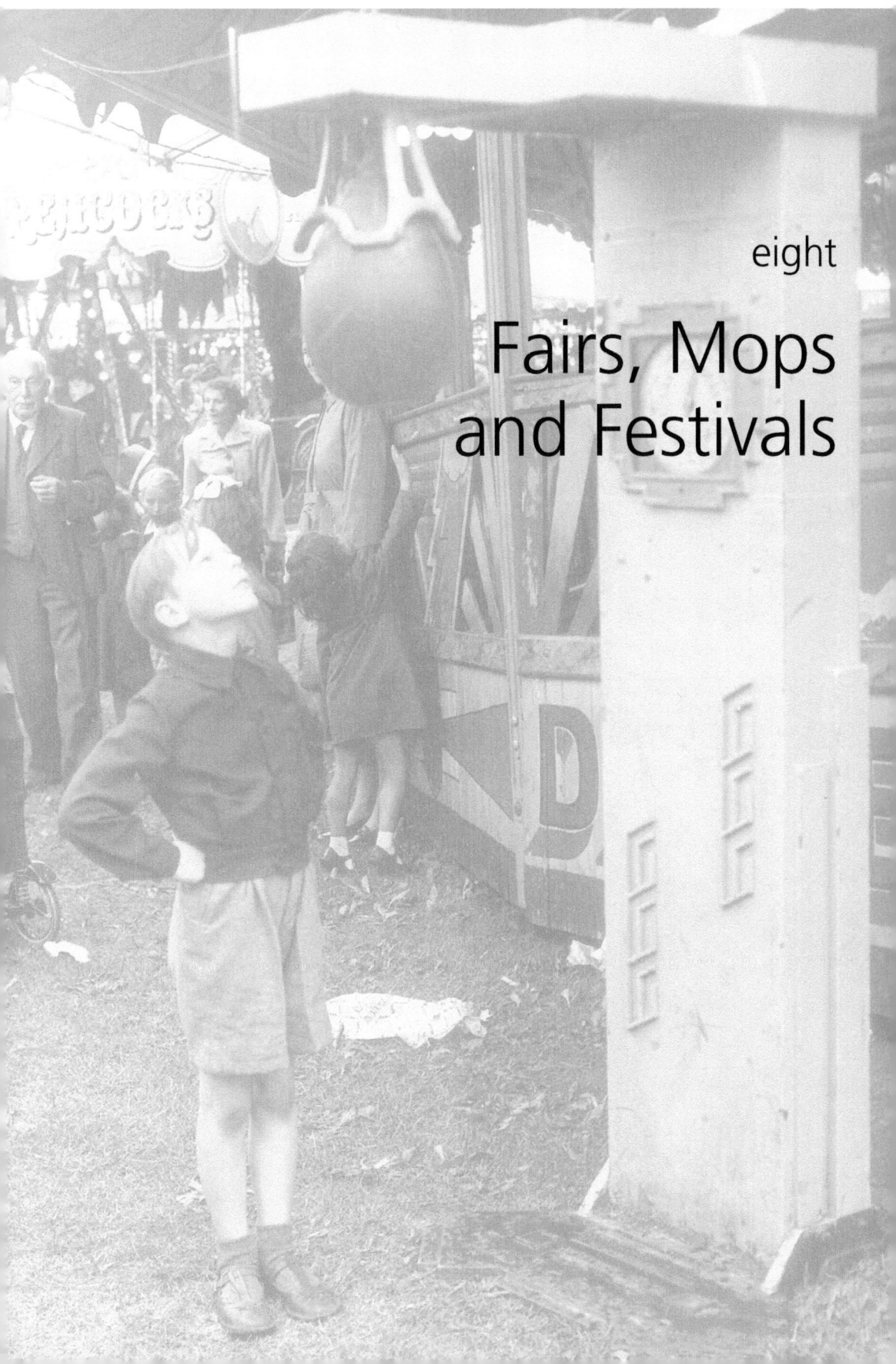

eight

Fairs, Mops and Festivals

Boys teasing horses at the horse fair, 1895.

Opposite above: At the horse fair near to the original St Catherine of Sienna Roman Catholic church, now Bristol Street, 1901.

Opposite below: Horses being sold at the horse fair, 1897.

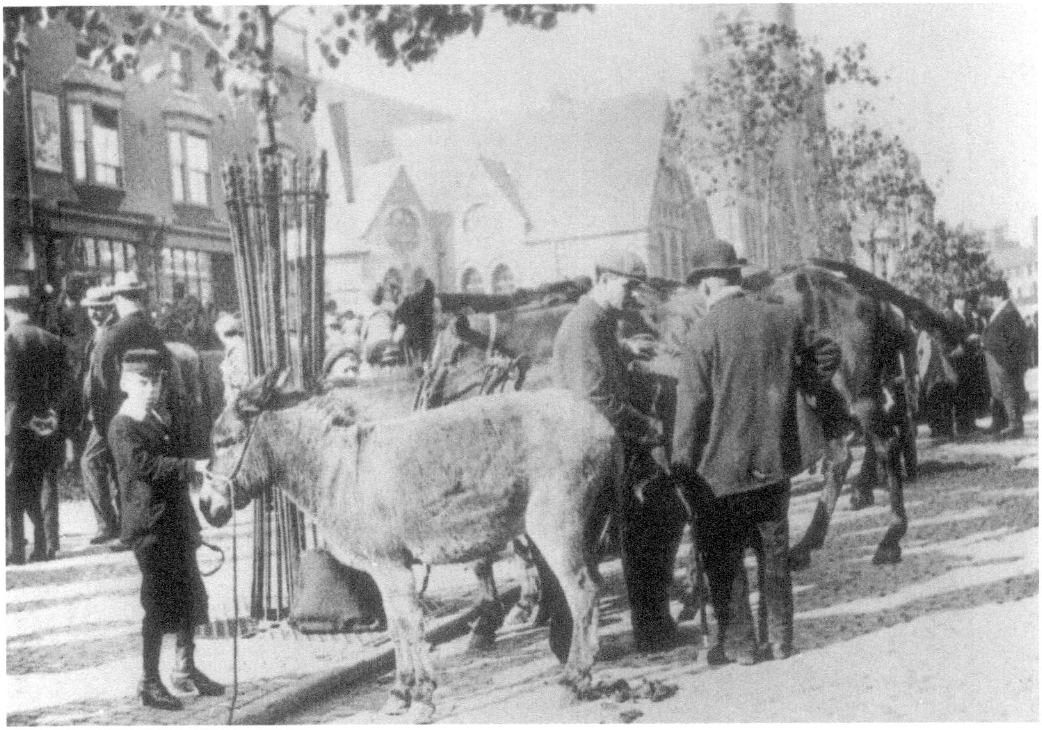

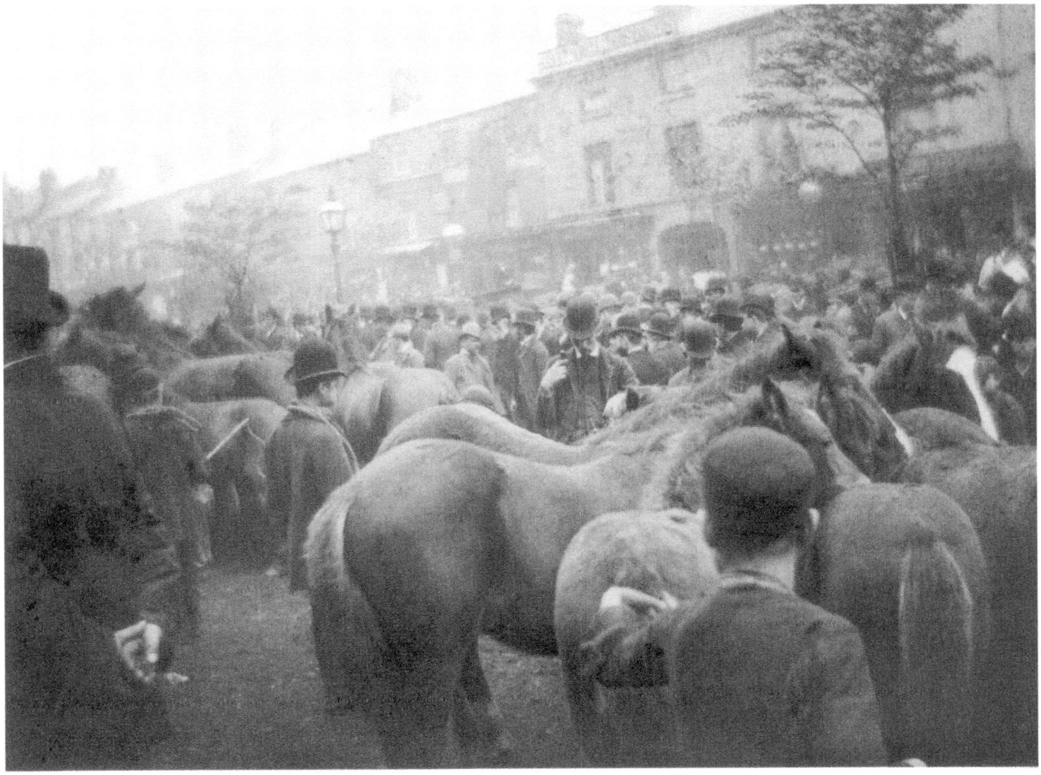

A mosaic of the horse fair, designed and produced by Kenneth Budd. This was situated in the underpass at Holloway Circus, close to the original horse fair, in 1980.

Young boys walking towards the onion fair at Aston, *c.* 1894.

An onion fair in Birmingham, *c.* 1874.

No comfort for a 'land-lubber' in this swinging boat, c. 1895.

Opposite above: A young couple enjoying watching the thrills and spills of the fair, Aston 1895.

Opposite below: Looking towards the roundabouts and swing boats at the fair, c. 1895.

A wonderful day at the fair for the whole family, *c.* 1874.

Families or members of the same family who made their living on the fairgrounds in the 1890s.

Above: For many years Pat Collins
and other showmen brought their
fairs into Birmingham, either at bank
holiday periods such as Easter and
August and also during the special
festivals such as the onion fair which
was usually held at the Serpentine
Grounds at Aston – where parts of
Aston Villa Club are situated now.
This toddler is reaching and touching
a toy monkey in the hope she will be
given it. The photograph was taken
at a fair at the Serpentine Grounds,
Aston, *c.* 1937.

Right: Show people prepare to put up
part of the show at the Serpentine fair
at Easter, 1937.

Pat Collin's men building the horse roundabout, *c.* 1949.

A frightening view from the big wheel at Aston, 1949.

A young boy, too small to hit the punch ball, ponders on ways of succeeding. Kings Norton carnival, 1953.

Left: All of the fun of the fair at the end of a helter-skelter ride, Aston, 1959.

Below: The thrills of the big wheel, Aston, 1959.

Right: Crashing into everyone on the dodgems, Aston, 1959.

Below: Trying to pick up custom on the rifle range, Aston, 1959.

Kings Norton 'Mop', 1895 – preparing to set up.

The traditional ox is being roasted at the wheelwright's shop at the rear of the Bull's Head Public House on The Green, King's Norton, during the 'mop' fair of 1898.

BIRMINGHAM
CENTENARY
CELEBRATIONS
1938

PAGEANT OF
BIRMINGHAM

ASTON PARK
11th to 16th JULY, 1938
PAGEANT MASTER - - *Gwen Lally*

ILLUSTRATED   SOUVENIR   BOOKLET   9^d

Through the years Birmingham has been involved in many festivals, some covering its own historical heritage, and some celebrating multi-cultural traditions. One such local event was the 'Pageant of Birmingham', held at Aston Park from 11 to 16 July 1938, celebrating the centenary of the Charter of Incorporation which made Birmingham a 'borough'. The affair was compered by Gwen Lally and literally hundreds of people, including many children, were involved. The pageant was strictly a grand affair and it told the story of Birmingham from pre-historic times. The photograph shows the cover of the illustrated souvenir booklet describing the pageant.

Breathing out clouds of smoke, in the dragon fashion, 'Egbert' – the pageant dinosaur – takes his first outing from the pageant workhouse in Cambridge Street.

Prehistoric families gather to have their photograph taken during the 1938 pageant.

Saxons and Normans begin to march.

King Henry II and Queen Eleanor of Aquitaine pause before handing over Birmingham's Market Charter during the pageant.

Famous actor/comedian Stanley Holloway enjoys attending a theatrical garden party during the run of the pageant. To the left is Mrs Cyril Abrahams of Moseley, and to the right Miss Gwen Lally, pageant master.

Almost fifty years later a not-quite-so-official pageant took place outside St Martin's parish church in the Bullring – the Digbeth Midsummer Festival of 1986; the band introduce the event.

The horseman stands guard.

The old and the new stand guard.

A 'medieval' Punch and Judy show takes place outside St Martin's church.

The 'Buzzard' man arrives.

A 'witch' is about to be burnt at the stake!

The band plays.

In the stocks.

A trumpet player at The Bullring Centre.

The Market Charter is read out.

Traditional Chinese 'lion dance' through Birmingham to celebrate the start of Chinese New Year, 1994.

nine

Circuses
and Kindred
Events

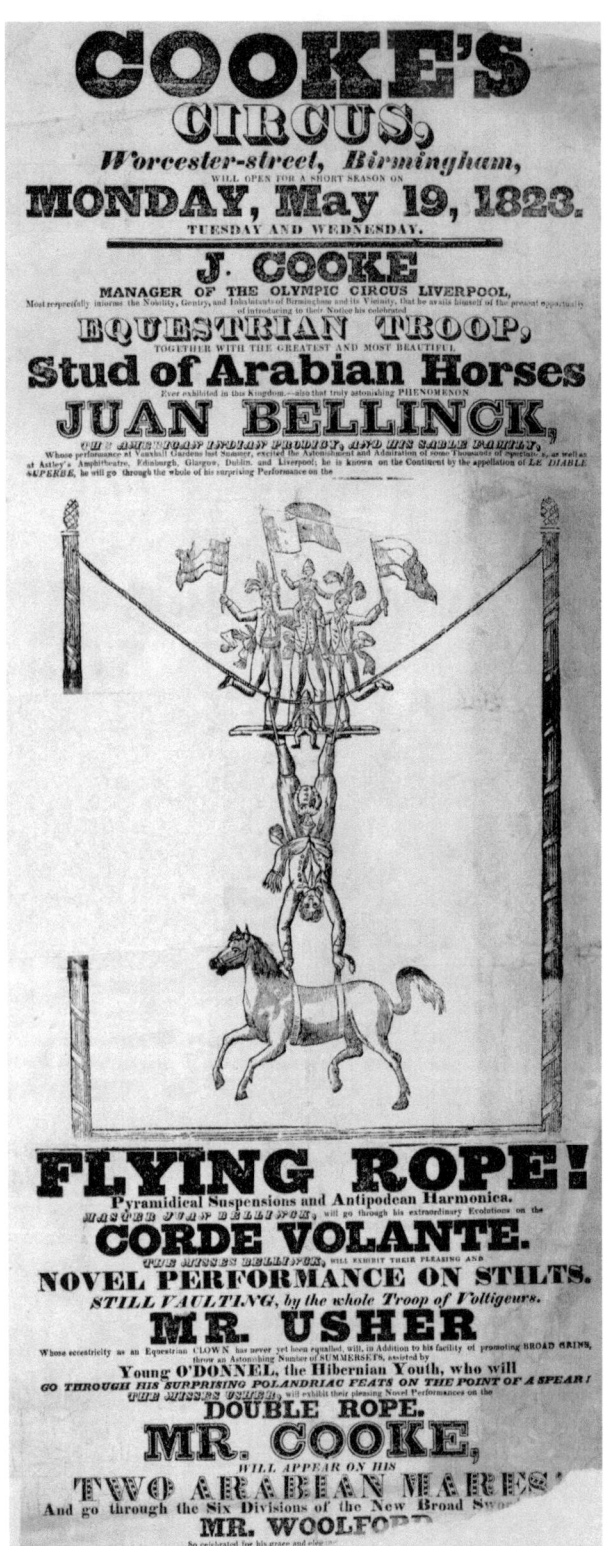

A poster advertising Cooke's Circus and an equestrian troop performing at Worcester Street on Monday 19 May 1823.

A poster advertising another equestrian circus taking part in the same week as above – Mr Lloyd's equestrian circus at Smithfield, 21 May 1823. 'Brummies' must have loved their horses.

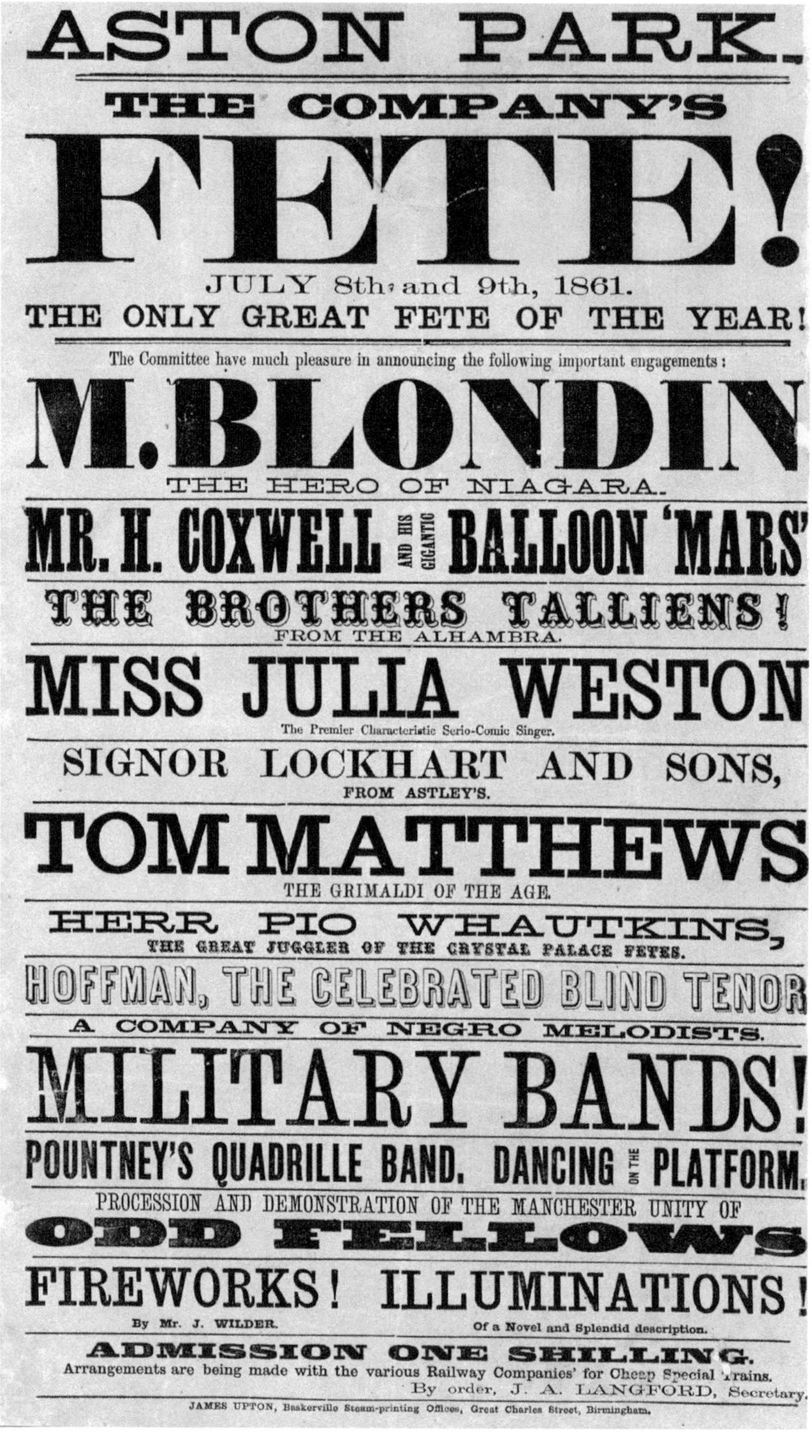

A poster advertising one of the most famous daredevil acts of the nineteenth century – the famous tight-rope walker, Blondin. This one informs us that he performed at Aston Park on 7 and 9 July 1861.

The front of a programme for a very popular circus that visited Birmingham regularly in the nineteenth century – 'Hengler's Grand Cirque' performing at Curzon Hall, Suffolk Street – later to be the area where the West End Ballroom and cinema was situated. This dates from 1892.

The actual programme of the above.

Barnum and Bailey's circus elephants trundling along Lichfield Road, Aston in 1899.

As part of the same company, camels belonging to Barnum and Bailey's Circus saunter along
Lichfield Road.

The elephants continue, but this time it is many years later in around 1951 and they are parading along the Coventry Road towards Hay Mills.

The crowds watching the parade are immense. At the time circuses were still extremely popular and no one thought that the animals were cruelly treated.

The big top site at the corner of New Street and High Street. The circus tent is being erected. The metal bars are in place but not the canvas, 1950s.

Almost completed.

Complete – showing other smaller tents and fairground stalls surrounding it.

Caravans on the big top site.

Buffalo Bill visited Birmingham on a number of occasions with his 'Wild West Show'. Here he is shown in formal pose.

Native American Indians.

A group of Mexicans line up in the parade.

Native American Indians parade along Corporation Street. This must have been a magnificent sight for the hundreds of people who lined the streets.

Even Cossacks join the procession.

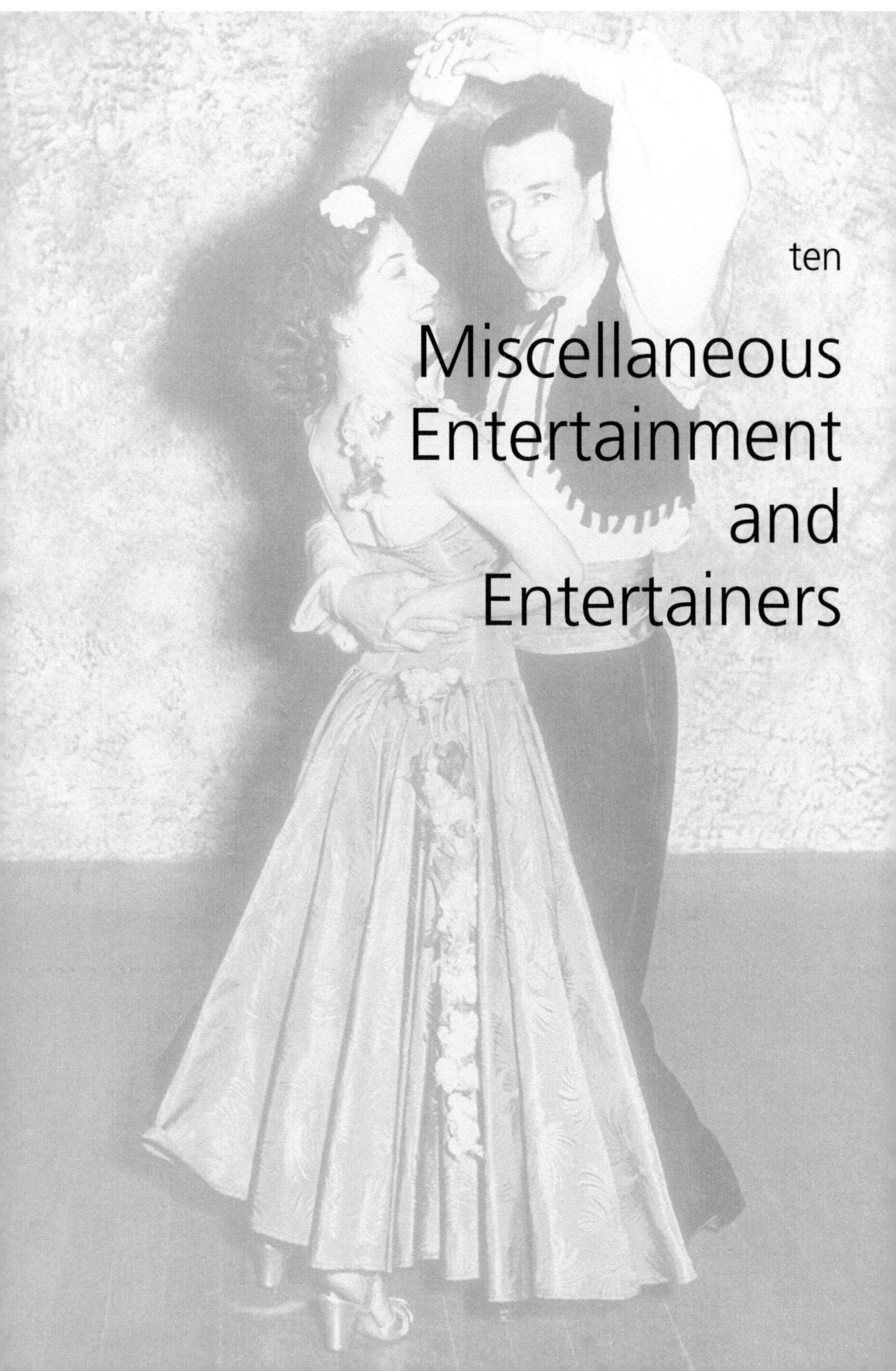

ten

Miscellaneous Entertainment and Entertainers

Above: MAC, Cannon Hill, founded by John English and Alicia Randle in conjunction with local politician Frank – later Sir Frank – Price. It was originally known as 'The Midlands Arts Centre for Young People', and was set in the grounds of Cannon Hill Park. It opened in 1962 and has continued as a successful venture, comprising theatre, cinema and areas for practical activities such as painting, sculpture and music. It is due to close in spring of 2008 for major refurbishment and will reopen in autumn 2009 in plenty of time to celebrate its 50th birthday in 2012. The photograph shows the Arts Centre as it was in 1966.

Left: Latin American dancing in Highfield Road, Hall Green with Henry and Mair Goodall, *c.* 1935.

Ballroom dancers at the Locarno Ballroom, Hurst Street 'strutting their stuff' in front of BBC television cameras for the extremely popular *Come Dancing* series in the 1960s.

Another popular entertainment was ice skating, and after the closure of the ice rink in Summer Hill Road in 1964 the Silver Blades Ice Rink in Pershore Street took over.

180mph on the streets of Birmingham as Formula 3000 cars roar down Belgrave Middleway. This photograph shows the Superprix of 1984.

Aerial views showing the International Convention Centre and Symphony Hall being built along Broad Street in the late 1980s. The centre was eventually opened by the Queen in June 1991. To the right, the Birmingham Repertory Theatre is very distinct.

A magnificent view of Birmingham and the now completed International Convention Centre, Symphony Hall and the Hyatt Hotel, distinctive as a result of its black appearance, 1991.

Shortly after the ICC began construction, work began on this building, situated just a few hundred yards away close to the canal – the NIA or National Indoor Arena, to give its official name. Now home to world-class indoor athletic events, concerts of all types, opera, and even the European Song Contest, this is another superb entertainments venue in Birmingham's cap.

Albert Ketelby. Ketelby was born in Alma Street, Newtown in 1875. He first began to compose music in the classical style, but became famous for descriptive popular works such as *In a Monastery Garden, In a Persian Market* and *Bells Across the Meadow*. He also distinguished himself as musical director of the Columbia Gramophone Co. and as a conductor. He died in 1959.

Michael Balcon. Balcon was born in 1896 and educated at George Dixon Grammar School, and although not strictly an entertainer, he was a pioneer of British films, most famous as the producer of a number of the great 'Ealing comedies' such as *Kind Hearts and Coronets, Passport to Pimlico, Whisky Galore, The Man in the White Suit, The Lavender Hill Mob* and *The Titfield Thunderbolt*. He died in 1977. His grandson is the oscar-winning actor Daniel Day-Lewis.

Left: Eric Maschwitz. Maschwitz was born in Birmingham; he was a waiter, novelist, reporter, and peanut-vendor in a French travelling circus. Maschwitz was to find fame as a librettist – writing the words for songs such as *These Foolish Things*, *A Nightingale Sang in Berkeley Square*, and for the musical *Summer Song* using the music of Anton Dvorak – as well as becoming head of television light entertainment for the BBC during its vintage years of *Hancock*, *Steptoe and Son*, *The Black and White Minstrel Show* and *Compact*. He was also at one time married to the actress Hermione Gingold.

Eric Maschwitz

Right: David Hughes. Hughes was born Geoffrey Paddison, in Bournbrook in 1925. After being demobbed from the RAF, David began his singing career in 1947. Record contracts and television shows made him a household name by the end of the 1950s, by which time he was known by his fans as 'Mr Heart-Throb'. By the end of the 1960s he had established himself in the opera world, appearing at Glyndebourne in 1964 (alongside Luciano Pavarotti), Scottish Opera, Welsh National Opera, The Royal Opera, Covent Garden and Sadler's Wells Opera (now English National Opera). On 18 October 1972, he collapsed on stage at the London Coliseum during a performance of *Madame Butterfly* and died the following day.

Bob Hatch. Hatch was regarded as one of Birmingham's most popular clubland comedians. He had appeared at London's famous Windmill Theatre and at The Birmingham Hippodrome, but it was in Midland clubland where he felt most at home. He died in 1975 in his fifties.

Alton Douglas. Another 'Brummie', Alton is today probably best known as the author of several best-selling books based on Birmingham and its neighbours, but he has also been a television quizmaster, comedian and actor, including appearances in virtually every major theatre in the UK. He has a wide variety of stories concerning his time as an entertainer, and one refers to him being accompanied by the worst organist he had ever heard. 'Where on earth did you get him from? I've never heard anything like it.' Alton enquired of the entertainment secretary. The reply came: 'Everyone says that – and we have to pay top money to stop the other clubs from poaching him!'

Laurie Hornsby. Hornsby, a very popular entertainer, was one-time guitarist and singer with groups such as The Exchequers and Varsity Rag. He is widely known today as the composer and librettist of two Birmingham-based community musicals *Wallop, Mrs Cox* and *Ridin' the No. 8*.

Derek Jacobi. One of the country's top actors, Sir Derek Jacobi spent a number of theatrical seasons in the 1960s at the original Birmingham Repertory Theatre in Station Street during the 1960s. He remembers whilst playing Shakespeare's *Henry VIII*, following one Wednesday afternoon's matinee, there was a knock on his dressing-room door and in walked Sir Laurence Olivier (himself a former Birmingham Rep actor), who offered him a job in his forthcoming Chichester season – a company that became the first National Theatre at the Old Vic – in October 1963, opening on the night of his birthday. Sir Derek stayed with Olivier for eight years.

Other local titles published by The History Press

Birmingham Shops and Shopping
PETER DRAKE AND ANDREW MAXAM

Like most big cities, Birmingham has lost many of its family-owned shops, department stores and Co-ops in recent decades. Illustrated with more than 190 photographs from the archives of Birmingham Central Library and from private collections, this book offers a unique glimpse into Birmingham's commercial past, capturing the diversity of Birmingham's shops and markets, and providing an important record of life in the city as it used to be.

978 07524 4493 2

King's Heath High Street A Nostalgic Journey
BOB BLACKHAM AND ANDY BISHOP

This fascinating selection of more than 200 archive photographs shows some of the many ways in which King's Heath has developed over the decades from the remote, rural origins that inspired its name, into a thriving suburb of Birmingham. Providing a rare insight into education, religion, drama at the Institute and literacy at the library financed by Scottish billionaire Andrew Carnegie, *King's Heath* explores every aspect of daily life in the town and will stir nostalgic memories in the minds of many residents.

978 07524 4481 9

Newtown and Summer Lane
PETER DRAKE AND JON GLASBY

References to Summer Lane and Newtown are rarely seen in published accounts of the city yet this area, close to the city centre, early a densely occupied one. This collection of images describes an area that has seen many changes and has been home to a large number of people. It will be an important record for those who have lived and worked there and it will put on the historical map an area that has until now been largely neglected by the historians.·

978 07524 4197

Birmingham and the Chamberlains
PETER DRAKE AND PAUL HARRIS

The Chamberlains are probably the country's best-known political family. Synonymous with Birmingham, they achieved both local fame and fortune and, with Neville's appointment as prime minister, the highest national office. Together, they transformed late Victorian Birmingham into 'the best-governed city in the world'. This work provides a fascinating insight into the Chamberlain's legacy, and will delight anyone who has lived or worked in the city.

978 07524 4492 5

Visit our website and discover thousands of other History Press books.

www.thehistorypress.co.uk